200+

Basic

Faith Activities for

Preschoolers

Also in the 200+ series

200+ Ideas for Teaching Preschoolers

200+ Games and Fun Activities for Teaching Preschoolers

200+ Things to Make for Teaching Preschoolers

200+ Ways to Care for Preschoolers

200+
Basic
Faith Activities for
Preschoolers

compiled by Rhonda Reeves

new
hope
PUBLISHERS

Birmingham, Alabama

New Hope® Publishers
P. O. Box 12065
Birmingham, AL 35202-2065
www.newhopepubl.com

Dewey Decimal Classification: 268.432
Subject Headings: Religious education—Preschool
                  Church work with youth

ISBN: 1-56309-801-6
N048105 • 0204 • 5M

Dedication

This book is dedicated in loving memory of Joni Johnson.
Joni worked with preschoolers and spent many years training preschool leadership
to know how to nurture faith development in our precious little ones.
She also wrote missions education materials for preschoolers, parents, and teachers.
Joni loved Jesus with all her heart and all her soul and with all her mind.
The life she lived was a beautiful reflection of Him.
Thank you, Joni, for letting His light shine in you!
We will always love and miss you!

Contents/Concept Areas

200+ Basic
Faith Activities for
Preschoolers

Chapter 1

GOD

God

If You Know . . .
To the tune of "If You're Happy and You Know It" sing:
> If you know that God loves you, clap your hands (clap, clap).
>
> If you know that God loves you, clap your hands (clap, clap).
>
> If you know that God loves you and you will tell somebody,
>
> If you know that God loves you, clap your hands (clap, clap).

Substitute the word *clap* with other motions (*stamp your feet, shout hooray,* etc.)

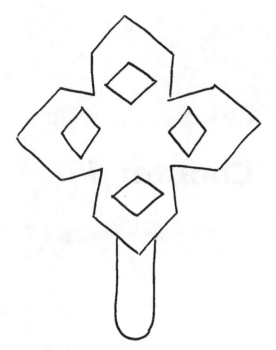

Snowflake Sticks

Snowflake Sticks
Materials: 6-inch squares of white paper, craft sticks, glue, scissors

Guide preschoolers to fold their squares of paper diagonally, then fold the resulting triangle in half. Cut a triangular piece from each of the three sides of the folded paper. Lead preschoolers to unfold their snowflakes and glue it to a craft stick. Say: God sends the snow.

Veggie Match

Veggie Match
Provide one green vegetable (cucumber, bell pepper, etc.); one orange vegetable (carrot, winter squash, etc.); one yellow vegetable (yellow pepper, corn, etc.); and one red vegetable (radish, tomato, etc.). Place each vegetable on a matching color of construction paper. Talk about the colors. Hold up each vegetable, and say: This carrot is orange. This cucumber is green. This corn is yellow. This radish is red.

Remove the vegetables and place in a small basket or box. Guide preschoolers to place the appropriate vegetable on the matching color of construction paper. Say: God gives food to us.

Bookmarks
Materials: colored construction paper, hole punch, ribbon or yarn, summer theme stickers

Print *God Loves You* on bookmarks. Lead preschoolers to place stickers on the bookmarks. Punch a hole at the top of the bookmark and thread ribbon or yarn through the hole.

Give each child a bookmark to take home to place in his favorite book or Bible.

For the Birds

Materials: two plastic margarine lids per child, 16-inch lengths of cord, birdseed, peanut butter

Punch a hole in the center of each lid. Guide preschoolers to place some peanut butter on the lids and then sprinkle birdseed on the peanut butter. Demonstrate how to tie a knot in one end of a cord. Lead preschoolers to thread the other end of the cord through the lid. Say: These tasty treats are now ready to hang in trees for our feathered friends!

Open the Bible and read: God made the birds (see Gen. 1:21).

For the Birds

Pattern Matching

In advance, cut poster board into 12-by-2-inch strips. Using 10 to 12 self-adhesive color dots per strip, place dots in various patterns on each strip (red, red, blue, blue, green, green, etc.).

Post the allergy alert chart on page 93 to inform parents of this tasting activity.

Place strips in the area along with a large bowl of small colored candies. Encourage preschoolers to choose a strip and place a matching color candy piece on each dot. Allow preschoolers to eat their candies when finished. Say: God made you to do many things.

Caution: This activity is for older preschoolers. To prevent preschoolers from eating too many candies, you may wish to limit their matching to 2 or 3 strips.

Open the Bible and read: God made us (see Psalm 100:3).

Pattern Matching

Make Pretzels

Materials: 1½ cups warm water; 1 envelope yeast; 4 cups flour; 1 teaspoon salt; 1 tablespoon sugar; coarse salt; egg; 2 bowls; measuring cup; measuring spoons; wooden spoon; cookie sheet; foil; vegetable spray; pastry brush; oven; allergy chart, page 93

In advance, make pretzels: Mix the water, yeast, salt, and sugar together. Then add the flour mixture to the yeast mixture. Knead 5 minutes. Cover and let rise until doubled. Divide the dough into individual balls. Roll each ball into a long rope. Twist each rope into a pretzel. Place pretzels on a cookie sheet lined with greased foil. Brush each pretzel with egg and sprinkle with salt. Let rise until doubled. Bake in preheated oven at 425°F for 12 minutes. Post the chart.

As preschoolers arrive, serve each child a pretzel. Thank God for good things to enjoy.

Fish Bowl

Pray for One Another

Teaching Tip: If time to make the pretzels is a problem, check the grocery store for large soft or hard pretzels.

Fish Bowl
Babies and younger preschoolers will enjoy watching a goldfish swim in water. Place the bowl in easy view of children, but use caution to protect the fish. Say: God made the fish (see Gen. 1:21).

Feeling and Touching Water
Materials: buckets or small tubs of water, small plastic cups, funnels, large spoons

If the weather is warm, plan an outdoor water activity. Place small buckets or dishpans of water and containers for measuring and pouring. Encourage preschoolers to pour water from one container to another and to feel the water pouring on their hands. Ask: How does the water feel when it touches your skin?

Say: Water is necessary for people, animals, and for plants to grow. God gives us water.
Open the Bible and read: God sends the rain (see Jer. 5:24).

Offer cool drinks of water to preschoolers. Children often prefer this to juice or a sweet drink.
Caution: Supervise carefully when preschoolers are near water.

Pray for One Another
Materials: newsprint, pictures of community and church helpers, hole punch, glue, ribbon, marker

Guide preschoolers to help you make a big book. Glue a picture of a community helper on each page. Above the picture print, *Pray for . . . .* Title the big book *Pray for One Another.* Punch holes in the pages and put together with the ribbon.

As a child looks at the book, say: This is a book about people you can pray for. Pray for the firefighter. How can you pray for the firefighter?
Open the Bible and read: Say thank you to God (see Psalm 136:1), and Pray for one another (see James 5:16).

Make an Orange Shake
Materials: 6-ounce can frozen orange-juice concentrate; ¾ cup milk; ¾ cup water; 1 teaspoon vanilla; ice cubes; blender; small paper cups; orange slices; measuring cup; measuring spoon; allergy alert chart, page 93

Have preschoolers wash their hands. Guide them to take turns measuring the ingredients and putting them into the blender. Add several ice cubes and blend until smooth and frothy. Pour into cups. Add a slice of orange.

Say a prayer before enjoying the snack to thank God for good things to enjoy.

Give Thanks
Materials: poster board, glue, markers, variety of nature stickers, collage materials

In advance, cut poster board into 2-by-8-inch strips. Print on the strip *Say thank you to God (see Psalm 136:1).*

Guide preschoolers to make a bookmark using the items. Talk to them about the importance of saying thank you to God. Ask each child to name something or someone for whom he is thankful. Suggest they share their bookmarks with a family member or friend.

Give Thanks

Catching Sun Rays
Materials: clear self-adhesive plastic, different colors of construction paper, colored plastic wrap, scissors, hole punch, ribbon

In advance, cut large circles out of the self-adhesive plastic, one for each preschooler.

Lead preschoolers to cut pieces of construction paper to place on the sticky side of the circle. When finished, help them put a piece of colored plastic wrap on top of the circle. Trim any excess. Punch a hole in the top of the circle, attach a piece of ribbon, and hang the decorated shape in a window observing what happens when the sun's rays shine on the decorated circle. Say: God made the sun.

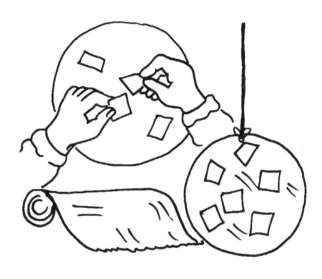

Catching Sun Rays

Digging for Treasure
Materials: two plastic dishpans, sand, assortments of shells and of rocks, plastic toy lizards, two buckets, two shovels, magnifying glass, pictures of a beach and a desert

In advance, fill both dishpans with sand. Bury the shells in one container of sand, and the rocks and lizards in the other container. Display the picture of the beach by the buried shells and the picture of the desert next to the buried rocks.

Invite one child to dig for treasure in the desert and another child to dig for treasure at the beach. When they have finished their "dig," talk about the treasures they found.

Open the Bible and read: God made the ocean and the dry land (see Psalm 95:5).

Under the Sea

Under the Sea
Materials: two paper plates per child; blue plastic wrap; markers; crayons; scissors; stickers of fish, seashells, sea creatures; sand; stapler

In advance, cut out the center of one plate for each child.

Guide each child to turn the rim right side up and put glue along the inside edge. Help her stretch a piece of blue plastic over the opening, gluing it to the rim of the plate. Cut away excess plastic. Next guide each child to place stickers and glue sand on the other plate. To finish the sea picture, place the plate rim upside down on the full plate and staple around the outside.

Open the Bible and read: God made the fish (see Gen. 1:21).

Corn Muffin in a Cup
Materials: corn muffin mix; measuring spoons; water; paper cups for hot drinks; spoons; electric skillet; allergy alert chart (p. 93); an ear of corn

Ask several preschoolers at a time to wash their hands and make a corn muffin. Guide each child to measure 3 tablespoons of corn muffin mix and 1 tablespoon of water in his cup. Stir together with a spoon until all ingredients are moistened. Place cups in an electric skillet with the lid on tight. Bake 350°F until done.

Show the boys and girls the ear of corn. Talk about how it grows and the different ways to eat corn: corn on the cob, corn bread.

Thank God for the good food He gives us to eat.

Floating Boats

Floating Boats
Materials: water table or plastic pan, plastic foam, toy boats, plastic fish, small plastic people figures, different sizes of plastic food containers

In advance, cut several island shapes from plastic foam. Float the islands in the water. Add the toy boats, fish, people, and food containers beside the water.

Invite a child to visit the area and use the boats to take the people to the islands. Explain that an island is land surrounded by water. Talk about ways to get to an island.

Open the Bible and read: God made the dry land (see Psalm 95:5).

6

Which Pocket?

Materials: tagboard; markers; colored construction paper; glue; pictures, such as elephant, hippo, rhino, crocodile, giraffe, chimp; small basket

In advance, cut out from colored paper the same number of "pockets" as animal pictures. On three of the pockets, draw a tree. On the other three pockets, draw a lake or river. Attach the pockets to the tagboard leaving an opening in the top of each one.

Place the animal pictures in the basket. Invite a child to select a card and tell something about the animal. He then places the animal picture in one of the pockets showing where the animal likes to be, land or water.

Say: God made the animals.

Blowing in the Wind

Materials: pieces of white poster board, washable markers, tape, crepe paper, string, hole punch

In advance, cut the poster board into fourths. Cut a diamond-shaped kite from each fourth. Or use the diagram (at right) to make five kites.

Give each child a kite shape. Guide him to decorate his kite with the markers. Help him tape crepe-paper streamers to the bottom corner of the kite. Punch a hole in the left and right corners. Thread a 36-inch length of string through the holes, tying a knot in the back of the kite, and leaving about 12 inches for the flying string. Say: Kite flying is a fun family activity. **Open the Bible and read:** God makes the wind blow (see Psalm 147:18).

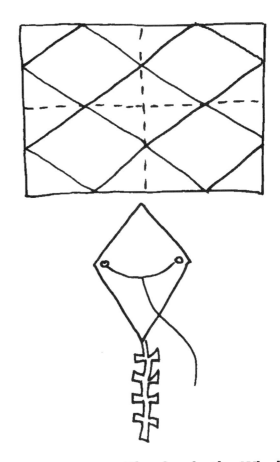

Blowing in the Wind

Glass-Bottom Boat

Materials: rope, seashells, fish shapes, clear plastic wrap, box, tape, container of water

In advance, make an outline of a boat on the floor using the rope. Cut a hole on opposite sides of the box, big enough for a child to put his hands through. Cover the box with plastic wrap. Secure to the box with tape. Collect objects that would be found in the ocean.

Invite preschoolers one at a time to sit in the glass-bottom boat. Guide a child to pour a small amount of water on top of the plastic wrap. The child chooses an object, places it through the holes, and observes. **Open the Bible and read:** God made the water (see Psalm 104:10).

Glass-Bottom Boat

Flower Puzzle

Ice Cream in a Bag

Materials: milk; sugar; vanilla flavoring; ice; salt; pint-sized plastic self-sealing bags; gallon-sized plastic self-sealing bags; paper cups; plastic spoons; allergy alert chart (p. 93); measuring spoons; measuring cup

Post the chart to notify parents of this activity. Guide boys and girls to fill the large bag half full of ice. Add 6 tablespoons salt. Seal the bag. In the small bag put ½ cup milk, ¼ teaspoon vanilla, and 1 tablespoon sugar. Seal the bag. Open the large bag, and place the small bag inside it. Seal the large bag and shake the bags until the mixture is ice cream. Take the small bag out of the large bag. Wipe off the top of the small bag. Then open very carefully. Pour ice cream into cups, and serve each child a small amount. Thank God for good food to eat.

Flower Puzzle

Materials: tagboard, pictures of flowers, clear self-adhesive plastic, marker, binding tape, scissors, glue

In advance, divide the tagboard into 16 sections. Glue a flower to the cross sections of the squares. Cover with clear plastic and bind the edges with tape. Cut out the squares.

Place the flower puzzle on the table. Invite a child to take the puzzle apart, mix up the pieces, and put it together again. Talk about the different kinds of flowers on the puzzle. Say: God makes flowers grow.

Tree Name Game

In advance, make an evergreen-tree game by cutting out a large tree shape from green butcher paper or poster board. Add a brown trunk. Tape to a wall. Print the name of each preschooler somewhere on the tree. Print the name of each preschooler on an index card.

Let preschoolers find their names, and match cards with the names on the tree. Use tape to attach the names to the tree. Read names. Say: God loves you, (child's name).

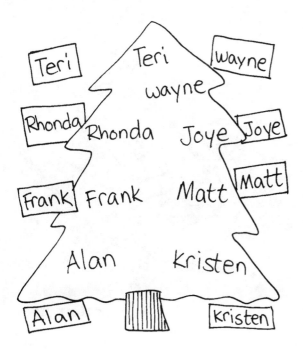

Tree Name Game

Crushed Ice Treat

Materials: blender or food processor; paper cups; fruit juice; ice cubes; plastic spoons; allergy alert chart (p. 93)

Post the chart to notify parents of this tasting activity. Guide each child to put ice in the blender or food processor to be crushed. After spooning the crushed ice into a cup, let him pour juice over the ice. Serve the crushed ice treat with a spoon.

8

Open the Bible and read: God is good to us (see Psalm 73:1).
Caution: Supervise carefully when preschoolers are near the blender.

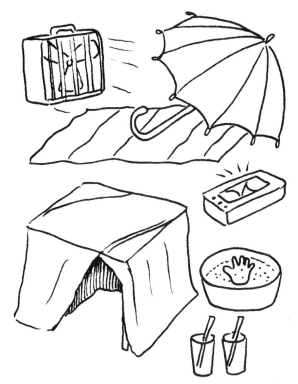

A Day at the Beach
Materials: beach towels, umbrella, container of sand, seashells, cold fruit juice, tape of beach sounds, floor fan with safety guard, blanket over a low table

Place the beach towels on the floor. Open an umbrella nearby. Turn on the fan, and play the beach sounds. Place several seashells in the area. Cover the table with a blanket. Say: Today we are going to the beach. We hear the waves breaking on the beach, and we hear and see seagulls. We feel the breeze blowing on our bodies. Let's pretend there is a cool cave under the blanket. We can go there when the sun gets hot. We can make hand-prints in the sand. Let's enjoy a drink of cold juice.
Open the Bible and read: God made the water (see Psalm 104:10).

Babies and toddlers will enjoy crawling under the blanket.
Caution: Post the allergy alert chart, page 93, to alert parents to tasting juice.

A Day at the Beach

Animal Movements
Gather pictures of the following: deer, armadillo, rac-coon, squirrel, snake, duck, turkey, pelican, fox, beaver, and alligator. Show preschoolers one of the pictures, and then lead them to move like that ani-mal. Be silly and have fun with the preschoolers. Say: God made the animals.

Seeing Stars
Materials: cardboard tubes, yellow cellophane, star stick-ers or paper cut into star shapes, rubber bands, crayons and markers

In advance, cut cellophane into circles one or two sizes larger than the cardboard tubes.

Guide preschoolers to decorate their telescopes. Next, have them place star stickers, or glue paper stars onto a cellophane circle. Help preschoolers place the cellophane circle on the end of a cardboard tube. Use a heavy rub-ber band to secure the circle.

Ask preschoolers what they see when they look through the other end of the tube.
Open the Bible and read: God made the stars (see Gen. 1:16).

Animal Movements

Fruit Salad

Materials: large bowl; fresh pineapple, bananas, guava, papaya; macadamia nuts; cutting board; butter knives; cutting knife; spoons; paper plates; allergy alert chart (p. 93)

Post the chart to notify parents of this activity. After hand washing, invite preschoolers to watch as you cut the fresh pineapple. Let them put the pineapple pieces in the bowl and pour in juice from the pineapple. As you skin or peel the fruit, let preschoolers use butter knives to chop the fruit into small pieces. Put away knives, and ask a child to stir the fruit salad. Ask for help serving salad to friends. Thank God for the good food. Enjoy the taste of fresh fruit.

Open the Bible and read: God gives food to us (see Psalm 136:25).

Stand-up People

Materials: pictures of culturally diverse people cut from old magazines, cards, newspaper, or catalogs; cardstock; glue; craft sticks; deep lids; plaster of Paris

Prepare stand-up people for preschoolers. Glue the pictures of people on cardstock. Attach a craft stick to the back of each figure. Follow package directions to mix plaster. Pour each lid full of plaster, and place a craft stick in each lid. Dry. Place in the area. Say: God loves people everywhere.

Food Book

Materials: small paper plates, scissors, glue, grocery store advertisements, hole punch, metal ring, marker

Ask preschoolers to cut out pictures of their favorite foods. Glue one food item on each paper plate. Label plates with food names and punch a hole in the top of plates. Spread the plates on the floor, and invite preschoolers to help you put the book in order. Use words like *first, second, then,* and *last.* Include a plate with the Bible thought written on it.

Open the Bible and read: Say thank you to God (see Psalm 136:1).

What Goes Together?

Materials: picture of a dog, cat, bird, and fish; dog bowl; cat bowl; fish bowl; bird water dish; self-sealing bags with a small amount of each pet's food; dog leash and bone; cat collar and mouse toy; plastic aquarium plant and gravel; bird mirror and perch

Stand-up People

Food Book

Place all items on a table. Invite preschoolers to find the items that go together. Ask them to name the items, and tell why they think each belongs to a certain animal. Identify items that are unfamiliar. Say: These are all pet things. Let's match the pet things to the pet.
Open the Bible and read: Everything God made was very good (see Gen. 1:31).

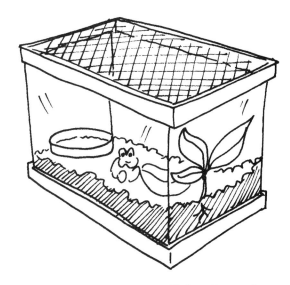

Build a Terrarium

Build a Terrarium
Materials: 10-gallon aquarium with a screen lid; aquarium gravel; soil; water; small plants; plastic frogs; water dish; allergy alert chart (p. 93)

Post the chart. Put a thin layer of gravel, and then several inches of soil on the bottom of the aquarium. Plant small houseplants in the soil, making sure all roots are covered with dirt. Put the shallow water dish in a corner (the pond). Fill the dish and water the plants. Add frogs, and lid. Say: Tiny tree frogs live in the rain forest. The coqui is a singing tree frog.
Teaching Tip: If available, show a picture of a coqui.
Open the Bible and read: God gives us things to enjoy (see 1 Tim. 6:17).

Going on a Squirrel Hunt
Materials: tissue tubes, masking tape, scissors, hole punch, yarn

In advance, make binoculars for each child. Tape two tubes together with masking tape. Punch holes in the top and make a loop with yarn.

Give each child his binoculars. Go for a walk and look for squirrels and other animals. Say: Thank You, God, for animals.

Horses and Play Dough
Materials: play dough (recipe, p. 22); rolling pin; plastic horses; craft sticks; plastic fences

Ask preschoolers to roll play dough flat. Show how to build fences for the horses. Let them walk the horses through the dough to make hoof prints. Encourage them to make things for the horses with play dough, such as a water tub, a bale of hay, jumps, and so on.

Painted Hearts
Materials: large paper heart shapes, easel, paintbrushes, paints in varying tints of pink and red, paint smocks

Invite interested preschoolers to come to the easel and paint a heart. (Be sure to help preschoolers put on a smock first to protect their clothing.) Say: A heart makes

Going on a Squirrel Hunt

us think of love. We want people to know that we love them. God also wants us to know that He loves us. He loves all people.

Open the Bible and read: God loves us always (see Psalm 107:1).

Bird Feeder

Materials: 3-ounce paper cups (non-waxed), glue or tape, spring-type clothespins, stickers, markers, birdseed

Invite preschoolers to decorate a cup with markers and stickers. Help them glue or tape clothespins to the sides of the cup. Show preschoolers how to fill the cup with birdseed and clip it to a tree branch or bush. Place in large plastic self-sealing bag so they can take the bird feeder home. Say: Thank You, God, for birds.

Bird Feeder

Singing Fun

Sing the following words to the tune of "Mary Had a Little Lamb":

I'm so glad that God loves me,
God loves me, God loves me,
I'm so glad that God loves me,
Yes, He does!

For variation, substitute names of individual preschoolers or toss a ball to a child and then sing the verse using that child's name.

Filter Flowers

Materials: three cone-shaped coffee filters, various colors of food coloring, ½ cup water, green chenille stems, small plastic bowls, paper towels, green construction paper, tape

In advance, cut a green construction-paper leaf for each child.

Mix water and food colorings in the bowls. Give each child three filters. Help preschoolers fold each coffee filter into thirds or fourths. Guide preschoolers to dip edges and corners of filters into the bowls. Unfold the filters and place on a paper towel to dry. After filters have dried, place them inside each other and pinch and twist at the bottom point. Attach a green pipe cleaner to make a stem. Use your fingers to shape the flower petals. Tape a green leaf to each stem. Say: God made flowers.

Filter Flowers

Beautiful Butterflies

Materials: paintbrushes, coffee filters, watercolor paints, bowl of water, spring clothespins, chenille stems, vinyl tablecloth

In advance, cover the work area with newspaper or a vinyl tablecloth.

Lead preschoolers to paint the coffee filter with watercolors. The colors will blend and mix into beautiful patterns. Give each preschooler a clothespin to paint, too. After filters and clothespins are dry, help preschoolers gather their coffee filters together in the middle and clip with the clothespin. Show preschoolers how to twist a piece of pipe cleaner around the clothespin to represent the antennae of the butterfly. Say: God made the butterflies.

Beautiful Butterflies

Scratch-and-Sniff Book

Materials: construction paper, water, powdered fruit-drink mixes, plastic bowls, paintbrushes

In advance, make a book for scratch and sniff pictures. Draw pictures of fruit on pieces of paper. These will become the pages of the book. Print the name of the fruit on each page. Make a book cover that reads *God gives us good food.*

Add 1 or 2 tablespoons of water to a package of powdered fruit-drink mix. Lead preschoolers to paint with the appropriate fruit-drink mixture to make fruits that actually smell like the picture they are painting. When the pictures are dry, show them how to scratch them with their fingernails to smell the fruit. Read the book together.

Open the Bible and read: God made the fruit (see Gen. 1:11).

Scratch-and-Sniff Book

Flannel-Board Book

Materials: one 3-ring plastic binder, paper-size flannel or felt pieces, glue, scissors, plastic page protectors, flannel-board pieces

In advance, glue the flannel or felt pieces to the inside of the binder. Cut off excess flannel. In plastic page protectors put different flannel-board pieces (Bible, flowers, people, etc.). Place these in the binder.

Invite interested preschoolers to take the flannel-board pieces from the page protectors and tell you a story as they place the pieces on the inside covers of the binder. Or if you prefer, you can tell a story to them.

Flannel-Board Book

Guest Guitarist

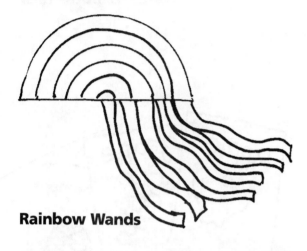

Rainbow Wands

Number Match

Guest Guitarist

Invite a church member who plays the guitar to come and visit the class. Ask the guest to explain how the guitar is played and to accompany the preschoolers as they sing a few praise choruses.

Open the Bible and read: I will praise God with a song (see Psalm 69:30).

Rainbow Wands

For each preschooler, cut a large paper plate in half, then cut off the rim of the plate. Lead preschoolers to color arches on the plate to resemble a rainbow. Staple or tape 12-inch lengths of different colored streamers to one end of the plate. Weather permitting, allow preschoolers to take wands outside and let the colors blow in the wind. Say: God made the wind to blow.

Number Match

Make an aquarium from blue poster board. Cut 20 identical fish from construction paper. Print two sets of numerals 1 to 10 on the fish (one numeral per fish). Glue one set of numbered fish swimming in the water. Cover with clear self-adhesive plastic. Cover the remaining set with wide plastic tape. Invite preschoolers to tell you the different numbers, and tape matching fish together in the aquarium. Count the fish. Say: People like to fish, look at fish, and eat fish for meals. God made the fish.

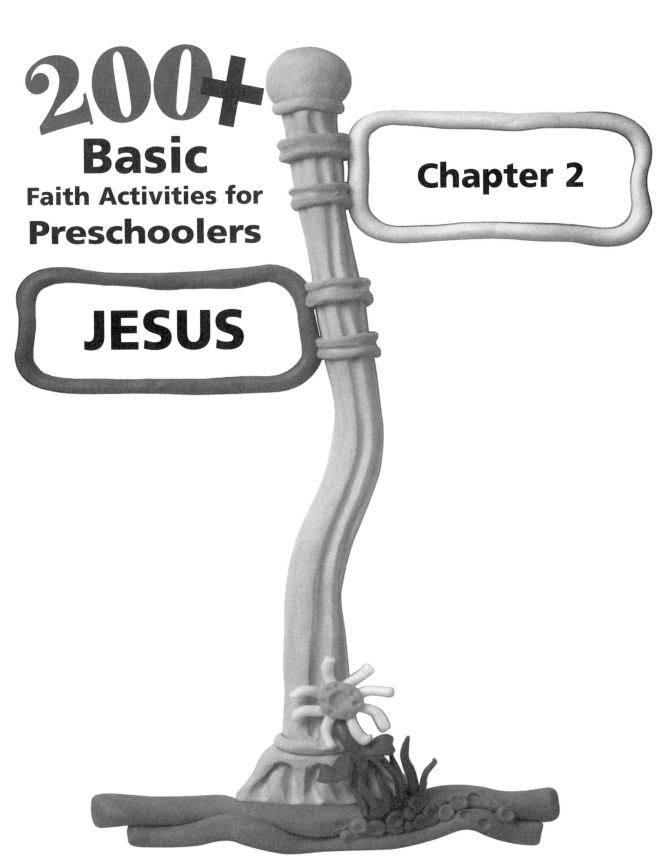

200+ Basic Faith Activities for Preschoolers

Chapter 2

JESUS

I Love Jesus and He Loves Me Booklets

These Are My Friends Booklet

Easy Puppets

Jesus

I Love Jesus and He Loves Me Booklets
Materials: construction paper, pictures of children and Jesus cut from old literature, glue

Give each preschooler two sheets of construction paper, and guide him to fold in half to make a booklet. Print *I Love Jesus and He Loves Me* on the front. Older preschoolers may wish to do this themselves. Lead preschoolers to glue pictures of Jesus and pictures of children on the pages of their booklets. Say: Jesus said, "You are my friends" (see John 15:14).

Rock and Read
Place child-size rocking chairs and an adult rocking chair in the area. Have several books about the birth of Jesus available for reading. Some preschoolers will want to "rock and read" by themselves. Be aware and make yourself available to those who will want you to "rock and read" with them. Remind preschoolers how glad you are that they are with you. Say: I love you. Jesus loves you, too.

These Are My Friends Booklet
Materials: construction paper, half sheets of copier paper, crayons, hole punch, yarn

Guide preschoolers to make a tracing of their hands on the copier paper, then write their names at the bottom of the sheet or on the hands. They will need to make a tracing for each of the friends in their class. Distribute hand tracings so that each preschooler has a tracing from everyone. Lead them to fold a sheet of construction paper in half for the cover. On the front, print *These Are My Friends*. Place hand tracings inside and punch holes down the side. Tie together with lengths of yarn.
Open the Bible and read: Jesus had friends (see Luke 2:52).

Easy Puppets
Materials: paper-towel tubes, yarn, markers, glue, fabric scraps or construction paper

Lead preschoolers to glue lengths of yarn to the top of a paper-towel tube for the puppet's hair, then draw faces with the markers. Using scraps of fabric or cut construction paper, guide preschoolers to glue on clothing for their puppets. Lead them to use their puppets to tell someone about Jesus.

Reversible Bracelets

Materials: poster board cut in 1-by-2-inch strips, hole punch, yarn, crayons

In advance, cut poster board into strips, then punch a hole at each end of the strip. Provide three strips for each preschooler. On one strip print *Jesus,* on another *loves,* and on the third *me.* Older pre-schoolers may do this themselves.

Guide preschoolers to use crayons to decorate the unprinted side of their strips, then using short lengths of yarn tie them together to make a bracelet. They may turn their bracelets facing the decorated side or the printed side. Say: These bracelets remind us how much Jesus loves us.

Reversible Bracelets

Baby Book

In advance, cut pictures of babies from magazines. Glue the pictures to colorful sheets of construction paper. Punch holes in one side and place in a ring binder or tie together with ribbons.

As you share this booklet with younger preschoolers, point out the expressions and activities of the babies in the book. Say: Jesus was a baby once. Jesus loves you.

Jesus Picture Book

Materials: pictures of Jesus cut from old preschool church literature, four paper plates per child, glue, crayons, hole punch, yarn

Guide preschoolers to glue pictures of Jesus to their paper plates. Lead them to decorate their plates with crayons. Punch two holes on the left side of each plate and tie together with yarn.
Open the Bible and read: Jesus went to church (see Luke 4:16).

Jesus Picture Book

School Help

Materials: preschool tablets, pencils, beginning reader books, alphabet cards

Lead preschoolers to role-play a tutoring program. Encourage older fives and prefirst to help younger preschoolers with writing and reading the alphabet.
Open the Bible and read: Jesus went about doing good (see Acts 10:38).

Autoharp Chorus

Materials: Autoharp, tape recorder, blank cassette

Wallpaper Place Mats

Use the Autoharp to accompany the preschoolers when they sing. Allow a few minutes for preschoolers to sing a favorite tune they have learned. Use a recorder to tape their music. Play it back later during listening time.

Babies and toddlers will enjoy moving or bouncing to the music. Say: Jesus loves (child's name) as you sing along.

Use music to soothe tired or sleepy babies.

Wallpaper Place Mats
Materials: roll of wallpaper (or large sheets of construction paper), markers, crayons, Bible-thought strips, paste

In advance, print the following Bible thoughts on colored strips of paper: *Sing thanks to God (see Psalm 147:7), God loved us and sent his Son (see 1 John 4:10), Pray for one another (see James 5:16), Jesus had friends (see Luke 2:52).* Cut place mats from the wallpaper.

Guide preschoolers to make a place mat for a nursing-home resident. Paste the Bible-thought strip on one side of the paper. Illustrate or color the design on the place mat. Discuss ways your preschoolers can help people in nursing homes (visit, sing songs, make a gift to give, send a card, pray and give money). Plan to take a group of preschoolers to visit a nearby nursing home to deliver their gifts.
Open the Bible and read: Jesus said, "Love one another" (see John 15:17).

Prayer Bookmarks

Prayer Bookmarks
Materials: 2 inch wide strips of construction paper, hole punch, short pieces of yarn, markers, candy canes

Look at the candy-cane stripes. Show preschoolers how to make stripes on their bookmarks. Let them punch a hole in the top and thread a piece of yarn through for a bow. On the back, print *Jesus prayed (see Matt. 14:23).*

Christmas Open House
Materials: Christmas tree, unbreakable ornaments, nativity figures, Bible

Open the Bible to the Christmas story (Luke 2). Engage the preschoolers in conversation about the figures.

Read the story from the Bible.
Teaching Tip: Invite family members to the class-

200+ Basic Faith Activities for Preschoolers

room. Serve cookies and sing Christmas carols. Then read the Christmas story from the Bible.

Listen to a Bible Story
Materials: tape recorder, blank tape, Bible, pictures of children of various ethnic groups

Record the Bible story of Jesus and the children from Luke 18:15–17. Place the Bible and the pictures of children near the tape player.

Summer Camp
Materials: tables, sleeping bags, backpack, craft items, blanket, clipboard, paper, tape player

Include the boys and girls in setting up a summer camp. Talk about the different things to do at summer camp, such as play sports, make crafts, eat, sleep, swim, hike, read, hear Bible stories, sing, and laugh and play with friends. Say: Some boys and girls who go to camp are deaf. The camp leaders sign with their hands when they talk to the deaf boys and girls.

Demonstrate how to sign *Jesus loves me*

Baby-Jesus Ornament
Materials: cardboard tubes, cut into 2-inch lengths (and then cut in half, creating two beds); yellow cotton balls; 1-inch baby dolls; 1-inch squares of flannel; thin ribbon; scissors; glue; hole punch

In advance, punch a hole in each side of the cribs.

Show preschoolers how to stretch and glue a cotton ball on the bottom of the crib (paper tube). Choose a baby, and glue it on the "straw." Select a "blanket" and glue to the baby. Let preschoolers cut a piece of ribbon, thread through the holes, and tie to make a loop. Say: Jesus was born in Bethlehem.
Open the Bible and read: Jesus was born in Bethlehem (see Matt. 2:1).

Plastic-Jar Book
Cut a piece of paper to fit the inside of a plastic gallon jar. Cover the paper with pictures of people (cut from magazines or newspaper ads). Print *Jesus loves you (see John 15:12)* on part of the paper. Place the paper inside the jar, and seal the lid. Set the jar on the floor. Lead babies and toddlers to look at the people.

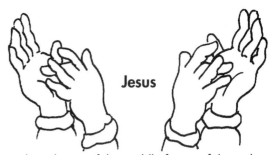

Jesus
Place the tip of the middle finger of the right open hand into the left palm and reverse.

loves
Open hands are crossed and pressed to the heart.

me
Point the right index finger at yourself.

Summer Camp

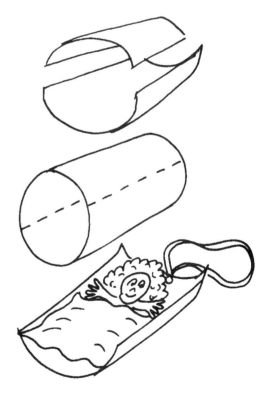

Baby-Jesus Ornament

Paper-Plate Wreath

Paper-Plate Wreath
Materials: paper plates with the centers cut out, green and red paint, paintbrushes, aprons, red ribbon bows, glue, tags with *God loved us and sent His son (see 1 John 4:10)* printed on them

Invite preschoolers to paint a plate green. Using a child's thumb, show them how to make red berries on the wreath. Attach a bow with glue. Attach Bible-thought tag to the wreath. Say: God loved us. He sent His Son, Jesus. Thank You, God, for sending Jesus.

Going to the Movies
Materials: chairs lined up like a theater, sheet attached to the wall, pictures of Jesus attached to the sheet, empty drink cups, paper sacks (pretend popcorn), tickets

Take a trip to the theater. Help preschoolers sell tickets, buy drinks and popcorn, and watch a movie (pictures of Jesus on the sheet).

Helping Others Back-to-School Supplies
Decorate a box to look like a school bus. Send home a note asking preschoolers to bring school supplies (pencils, paper, notebooks, crayons, glue, scissors, and so on) and place them in the box. Tell preschoolers that the school supplies will be given to a needy family or to a shelter for women and children.

Open the Bible and read: Jesus went about doing good (see Acts 10:38).

Autograph Book
In advance, make an autograph book with half sheets of construction paper. Staple several pieces together along the short edge. Print *Autograph Book* on the front. Add a picture of each preschooler, one per page. Draw a speech bubble on the top of each page, leaving room on the bottom for preschoolers to autograph their names. Include a picture of Jesus on one page, with a speech bubble that says *I love you.*

As preschoolers write their names, fill in the speech bubble with what they say. Share the book.

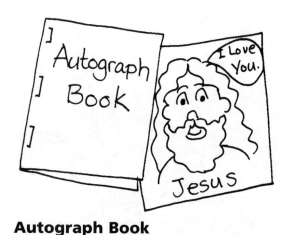

Autograph Book

People Floor Puzzle
Materials: magazine pictures of people, poster board

In advance, make a people puzzle. Cut out pictures of people of all ages and ethnic groups from

20

old magazines. Glue these to a piece of poster board to make a montage of people. Cut the poster board into 6 to 8 pieces.

Lead preschoolers to put the pieces together. Say: Jesus loves all these people. Jesus loves you, too.

Sing "Jesus Loves Me."

Accordion Heart Book

Materials: large pink or red construction paper, markers, crayons, stickers

In advance, fold construction paper in half. Cut the folded paper into the shape of a large valentine heart. Then fold the heart accordion-style, so that it has four panels. On page one, print *Jesus loves me.* On page two, print *I love Jesus.* On page three, print *I love my church.* On page four, print *My church loves me.*

Give each preschooler a heart-shaped accordion book. Encourage them to draw pictures or add stickers to each page. Say: Jesus loves you. Jesus loves me. Jesus loves all people. Your church loves you. **Open the Bible and read:** Jesus loves you (see John 15:12).

Milk-Carton Book

Cover a clean half-gallon cardboard milk carton with construction paper. On one side, put a picture of your church, and under it print *Jesus went to church (see Luke 4:16).* On the next side, put a picture of Jesus, and under it print *God loved us and sent his Son (see 1 John 4:10).* On the next side, put a picture of all of your preschoolers, and under it print *Love each other (see John 15:17).* On the last side, put a picture of the Bible, and under it print *Jesus taught the people (see Luke 5:3).*

Read the milk-carton book with preschoolers.

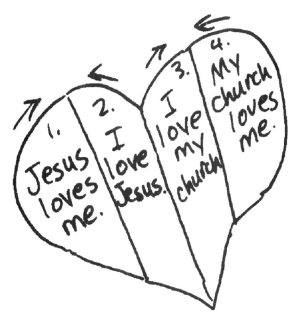

Accordion Heart Book

Milk-Carton Book

ART RECIPES

Play Dough Recipe

    3 cups flour
    1 cup salt
    1 tablespoon alum
    2 tablespoons oil
    food coloring
    3 cups boiling water

Mix together all ingredients except water and coloring.

Put food coloring in measuring cup, and add water to it.

Pour water in with other ingredients.

Mix and knead well.

Store in a covered container until ready to use.

Here is a fun recipe to make with preschoolers.
Goop Paint

Mix together one part salt, one part flour, and one part water in a bowl. Stir the mixture until it is smooth, then pour it into several empty glue bottles. Add a few drops of food coloring or tempera paint to each of the bottles to create a variety of colors. Attach the caps and shake well. Shake before each use. This paint will give your projects a "glittery" look.

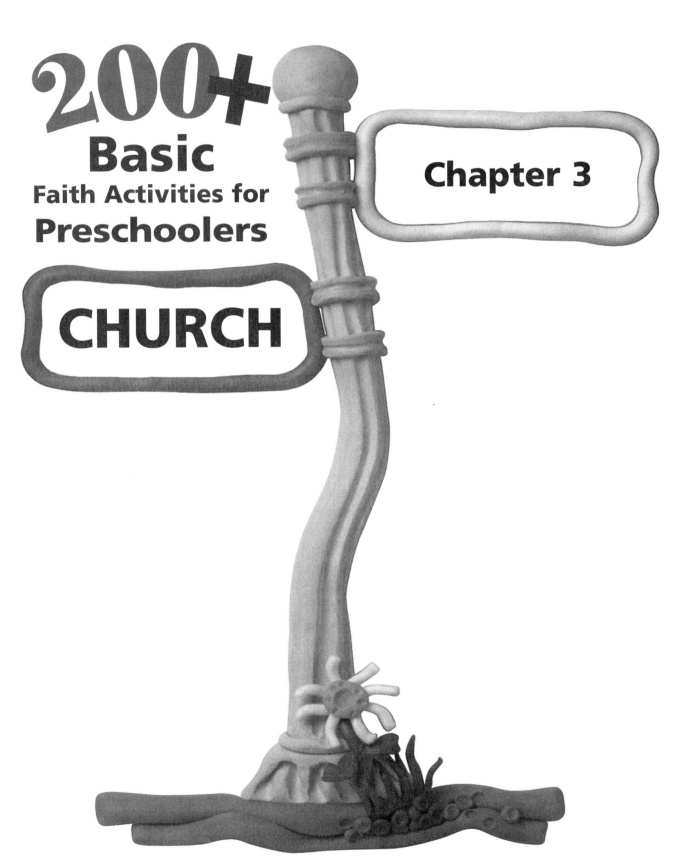

200+ Basic Faith Activities for Preschoolers

CHURCH

Chapter 3

Church

Touch Match

Touch Match
On 10 or 12 large blank index cards, glue identical designs of yarn patterns on each pair of cards. Display half of the cards, and stack the other half facedown. Place one card from the stack in a box, bag, or other container. Guide preschoolers to reach inside the container without looking, feel the pattern on the card, and indicate the matching card on display. Verify his guess by placing the card from the container beside the display version. Say: We have fun at church.

Helping Others Thank-You Tree
In advance, photocopy leaves on page 34. Provide a thin tree branch for preschoolers to tie their leaves onto. Place the tree branch in a medium-sized plastic flowerpot filled with sand.

Lead preschoolers to color their leaves and tie them onto the "tree" with yarn. Discuss to whom you will give the tree. Talk about the ways that person helps in your church. Say: Thank You, God, for

_____.

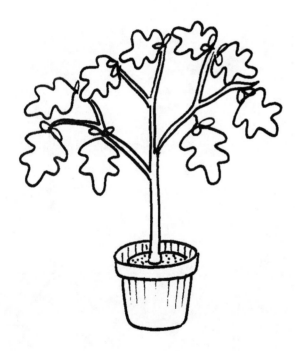

Helping Others Thank-You Tree

Bangle Bracelets
In advance, begin saving the plastic rings from six-pack beverages. Cut apart each six-pack holder to make six circular rings.

Guide preschoolers to use different colors of glue to decorate a plastic ring to make a beautiful bracelet. **Open the Bible and read:** I like to go to church (see Psalm 122:1).

Money Bags
In advance, gather enough pieces of white felt so that each child can have two rectangular pieces approximately 4-by-6 inches.

Provide plastic sewing needles and yarn. Thread each needle and guide preschoolers to sew the sides and bottoms of the felt pieces together. Leave the top of each bag open,

Provide several different colors of fabric markers. As preschoolers decorate their bags, talk about how their money helps others.

Bible-Thought Sentence Strips

On sentence strips print each of the following Bible thoughts: *Bring an offering to church (see Mal. 3:10); Bring an offering (see 1 Chron. 16:29); God loves a cheerful giver (see 2 Cor. 9:7); We work together (see 1 Cor. 3:9); Help one another (see Gal. 5:13); and We are helpers (see 2 Cor. 1:24).* At the end of each sentence strip use a marker to color code it. Place the strips around the room.

Place colored construction-paper strips in the Bible to match the appropriate color sentence strips. As a preschooler discovers a sentence strip, read the Bible thought to him. Talk about what each Bible thought means, and then ask the child to find the matching color strip in the Bible. Read the verse from the Bible. Remind preschoolers how giving money to help the church helps in many ways.

Bible-Thought Sentence Strips

Making Banks

Here are several variations for making banks. After making a bank, encourage preschoolers to place extra coins they may have in their banks. Then remind them to give the money in their banks to their church. Remind them that their money goes to help in many ways. Talk to the preschoolers about how their money helps as they are making a bank.

Tub Banks

In advance, cut a slit large enough so coins will fit through in several margarine tub lids.

Give each child a lid, and encourage him to place it back on the container. Provide scraps of paper or fabric, yarn, ribbon, and rick-rack and lead preschoolers to glue the items onto the containers. Give each child a coin to drop in his bank. Encourage him to save money at home and bring the money he saves back to church and give it to help others.

Making Banks

Papier-Mâché Bag Banks

Give each preschooler a lunch-sized brown paper bag. Encourage them to open up their bags and stuff them full with small newspaper balls. Help each child to use masking tape to wrap around the opening of the bag to keep the newspaper balls inside. Then lead preschoolers to tape around the remainder of the bags for support.

In a large plastic bowl help preschoolers mix flour and water to make a thin paste. Give each preschooler several newspaper strips and lead him to soak his strips in the paste and then smoothly place them around the bag. Help preschoolers cover their bags completely with the pasted strips. DO NOT place strips around the opening of the bag. Allow the bags to dry at least 24 hours.

When the bags are dry, remove the newspaper balls inside the sack. Pour several different colors of tempera paints into separate pie tins. Suggest preschoolers paint their bags, and then allow to dry. On self-adhesive name tags print each child's name. Underneath his name, print *My Money Helps*. Place the name tags on the bag. Be sure the openings of the bags are facing upwards. Encourage preschoolers to drop their money into the Bag Banks.

STOP and Think—Money Matters

In advance, make a stop sign by cutting a piece of cardboard into a circle. On the circle, write STOP in big letters. Glue the circle to either a broomstick or yardstick.

Give each child some play money. Hold up the STOP sign and ask each child to STOP and think about ways his money could help others. Lead him to divide up the money and tell how he would use it to help others. Be sure if the child forgets to include giving some of the money to church that you remind him that he might give some of his money to the church.

A Cheerful Giver—Sing Along

Lead preschoolers to sing the following song to the tune of "London Bridge":

A cheerful giver I will be.
I will be. I will be.
A cheerful giver I will be.
Makes God happy.

Giving money to my church,
To my church. To my church.
Giving money to my church.
Makes God happy.

Work together, my friends and me.
Friends and me. Friends and me.
Work together, my friends and me.
Makes God happy.
Repeat the first verse again.

STOP and Think—Money Matters

Sewing

Materials: poster board, hole punch, lengths of yarn, masking tape

In advance, cut poster board into simple shapes of T-shirts, dresses, and blankets (squares). Around the edges of each piece, punch holes all the way around. Wrap masking tape around one end of a long length of yarn for the needle.

Guide preschoolers to "sew" their cards by taking the yarn in and out of the holes. Say: As we sew, tell me what you like to do at church.

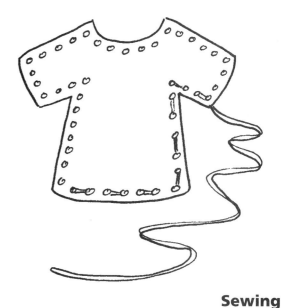

Sewing

Helping Others Welcome Mugs

Ask church members to donate coffee mugs from home (scenery or floral designs). Ask parents to send a bag of individually wrapped candy. Gather church business cards, candy, cups, tea bags, tissue paper, curling ribbon, scissors, and welcome notes.

Help preschoolers fill mugs with candy, a business card, a tea bag, and a note. Wrap each mug with paper and tie with ribbon. Give welcome mugs to guests on Sunday morning.

Note: If possible, arrange for preschoolers to deliver mugs to guests during the service.

Being Different Yet Part of a Group

Help preschoolers understand the concept of being unique and different, even when they're part of a group. Lead them to sing a song asking one child to sing one word, another child the next, and so on. Then have them sing the song together listening to see if they can hear each other's voices. Ask: Can you hear the others singing when you sing? What would happen if each of us talked at the same time? Could we hear each other?

Suggest preschoolers all talk at once. Say: See. It's hard to understand what you are saying unless everyone is listening to you isn't it?

Continue: All the people in our church are different, but they are also alike. We are all members of our church. Members of a church work together. When we work together, we can help others learn about Jesus. Listening to each other and learning from others is important.

Open the Bible and read: We work together (see 1 Cor. 3:9).

Helping Others Welcome Mugs

The name of my church is York Terrace Baptist

My Pastor's name is brother Knight

My teacher is Mrs. O'Conner

My friends

This is what I like best about church

My church by Linda Barnes

My Church Booklets

Build a Church

My Church Booklets

On sheets of white copier paper, print a statement about your church at the bottom. (For example: *The name of my church is ___; My pastor's name is _____; My teachers are _____; This is what I like best about church; etc.*) Make a copy of these sheets for each preschooler.

Lead preschoolers to illustrate the pages of their booklets. Provide sheets of construction paper to use as a cover. Print *My Church* on the front. Say: I'm so glad you came to church. Thank You, God, for our church.

Build a Church

Materials: toolbox, set of toy tools, hard hat, ruler, cardboard stacking blocks

Explain the stages of building construction. Ask preschoolers to name types of buildings they have seen being built. As preschoolers use the items to build, say: Some people travel to help missionaries build churches. Building a church takes teamwork.

Use the following as a way to show how everyone's job is important:

Who works to draw the plans for the church?
The architect works to draw the plans.

Who works to build the frame for the church?
The builder works to build the frame.

Who works to install the plumbing in the church?
The plumber works installing the plumbing.

Who works putting electrical wires in the church?
The electrician works to put in the wires.

Who works to build the walls of the church?
The builder works to build the walls.

Who works to paint the church?
The painter works to paint the church.

Who goes to church?
We do! We do! At church we work together!
Teaching Tip: Provide props representing each job.

Building Churches

Materials: cardboard box, large nails, small hammer, soft board, tool apron

In advance, begin several nails in the board. Place the box with the tools nearby.

Encourage preschoolers to pretend they are building a church.

Shadow Puzzle

Materials: objects found in the classroom, such as a crayon, pencil, block, book, toy, puzzle piece; poster board; black marker; small basket

In advance, arrange objects on a piece of poster board. Using the marker, trace around each object's shape. Laminate for durability.

Guide a child to take an object from the basket and match it to the corresponding shape on the poster board. Identify each item and how it is used in the classroom. Say: You can be a helper at home and at church. How can you help at church?
Open the Bible and read: Help one another (see Gal. 5:13).

Shadow Puzzle

Build It—What a Big Church

Guide preschoolers to use the blocks to build churches. As they work, say: When we come to our church, we can give money. This money goes to help others in our community and in other places far away. Thank you for wanting to give money to your church.
Open the Bible and read: God loves a cheerful giver (see 2 Cor. 9:7).

Helping Others Heart Baskets

Make heart baskets by cutting out heart shapes from construction paper. Roll the hearts into a cone shape and staple. Punch holes and attach a ribbon for a handle. Fill with candy. Add a note that says *Thank you for all you do.*

Give a heart basket to each staff member at church.
Open the Bible and read: Be kind to each other (see Eph. 4:32).

Helping Others Heart Baskets

Row Your Boat

Bring a pair of real oars and place on the floor. Invite preschoolers to get in the boat and row. Sing "Row, Row, Row Your Boat" as you move the oars. Sing another verse about going to church.

Go, go, go to church, learn and sing and play.
Families like to go to church.
Show your friends the way.

Open the Bible and read: I like to go to church (see Psalm 122:1).

Magnetic Car

Magnetic Car
Materials: tagboard, car pattern on page 34, magnet, paper clips, scissors, small box

In advance, trace the pattern of the car on the tagboard (stickers or pictures from magazines can be used). Cut out the picture of the car. Attach a paper clip to the backside. Draw lines on one side of the box for a highway.

Invite a child to hold the car up on the side of the box that has the highway. Another child holds the magnet on the other side of the box. As she moves the magnet on one side of the box, the magnet will move the car along the highway on the other side. Say: Some people come to church in a car. How do you come to church?
Open the Bible and read: I like to go to church (see Psalm 122:1).

Bible Story
In advance, locate one or two colorful pictures of the Bible story of Mary and Joseph taking Jesus to church. Place a quilt on the floor and leave the pictures and a Bible nearby.

Sit on the quilt. When interested preschoolers come to you, briefly tell them the Bible story. Show the pictures as you tell the story. When finished, say: That was a good Bible story, wasn't it? I'm glad you came to church just like Jesus did. Thank You, God, for our church.
Open the Bible and read: Jesus' family went to church (see Luke 2:27).

What's in the Bag?
Materials: two apples, two oranges, two cans of soup, pair of mittens, two hats, pair of shoes, pair of socks, shopping bag

Put the items in the shopping bag. Guide preschoolers to take turns removing one object at a time from the bag. As they match the pairs of objects, place them together. Say: Church members can provide food and clothes for people in the community who need them. Church members can invite the people to church.
Open the Bible and read: Be kind to each other (see Eph. 4:32).

What's in the Bag?

Driving to Help

Materials: toy vehicles, wooden blocks, traffic signs

Help preschoolers pretend they are driving to a church. Provide toy vehicles for the preschoolers to "drive" and traffic signs (Stop, Yield, etc.) to use. Encourage preschoolers to build churches with wooden blocks. As preschoolers play, talk about all the ways people might travel to their church building.

Teaching Tip: Purchase traffic signs at either toy or teacher stores. If you prefer, make your own traffic signs or let preschoolers help you make them. Cut out the shape of the sign from construction paper. Tape the sign to a craft stick and then place the bottom of the stick into clay so it can stand.

Driving to Help

You're Invited!

Materials: colorful cardstock paper cut in half; stickers; markers; glue; variety of art supplies (buttons, yarn, fabric scraps)

In advance, type or print information about your church's worship services and opportunities for service. Photocopy the information for each child.

Guide preschoolers to fold a piece of cardstock paper in half to make a card. Help them glue the church information inside the card. Preschoolers can decorate the cards with art materials provided. Ask: Can you think of someone you could invite to church?

Write a Song

Materials: newsprint, markers

Write a song about church helpers. Ask preschoolers to name a church helper and something that is part of his job, such as the custodian vacuums the floors or the choir director leads the music. Print the words as the preschoolers dictate. When the song is complete, let the preschoolers draw pictures illustrating the church helpers and the jobs they do.

Invite the minister of music or another church helper to visit and talk about the work he does at church.

Church-shaped Books

Church-shaped Books

Materials: paper cut in the shape of a church, markers or crayons, stapler, staples

Give each preschooler one church-shaped paper. Guide preschoolers to draw a picture of something about their church. Ask each preschooler to tell you

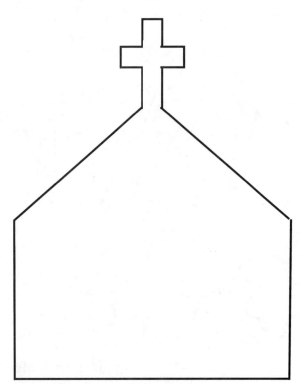

Church Scavenger Hunt

Stained-Glass Windows

about his picture, and print a sentence on each page. Assemble all the pages together into a book and staple. Read the book to the group. The title might be *I Like To Go To Church* or *Thank You, God, for My Church.*

Church Scavenger Hunt
In advance, hide church-shaped cutouts in various places around the church building (classroom, choir room, sanctuary, office, library, etc.).

Take preschoolers on a walk through the church. As they walk, ask them to look for the church-shaped cutouts you have hidden. Explain to preschoolers how different areas in the church building are used.

Stained-Glass Windows
Materials: waxed paper, cotton balls, salad oil, tissue paper, black construction paper, scissors

Have preschoolers dip cotton balls into salad oil and brush them over waxed paper. Then lead them to tear tissue paper into little pieces and press them all over the waxed paper until it is completely covered. (The oil helps the tissue paper stick to the waxed paper and makes the tissue paper translucent.) When the picture dries, add a black construction-paper frame to create a stained-glass window.

As preschoolers work on this project, explain that churches meet in many different places. Say: Some churches meet in old, large buildings with stained-glass windows. Others meet in someone's home or even in a storefront.

Thank-You Books
Materials: construction paper, drawing paper, stickers, markers, crayons, stapler, staples

Say: We have special people who help us at our church, too. Can you think of some of these people?

Help preschoolers name some of the helpers at your church. Lead them to choose one or two helpers to whom they would like to give a thank-you book.

Older preschoolers can work in small groups. Give each child a piece of drawing paper. At the top of the page, print the following phrase: *(Preschooler's name) is thankful that you help our church.* Encourage preschoolers to use provided materials to draw a picture or decorate the page. Staple all the pages together to create a thank-you book. Allow preschoolers to deliver the book or ask the special helper to visit the room to accept the thank-you book.

Open the Bible and read: Help one another (see Gal. 5:13).

Bulletin Board

Cover a bulletin board with blue paper. Make a large brown apartment-style church in the center, with a cross on top, and double doors at the bottom. Make window flaps by cutting gray squares from construction paper, and drawing pane lines with a marker. Tape enough windows on the church (tape along the top edge only) to have one for each preschooler and teacher. Place a picture of each child and teacher, one under each window flap, on the bulletin board. Print *Look who goes to church!* at the top. Across the bottom, print *I like to go to church (see Psalm 122:1).*

Thank-You Books

Bulletin Board

Leaf Patterns

Magnetic Car Pattern

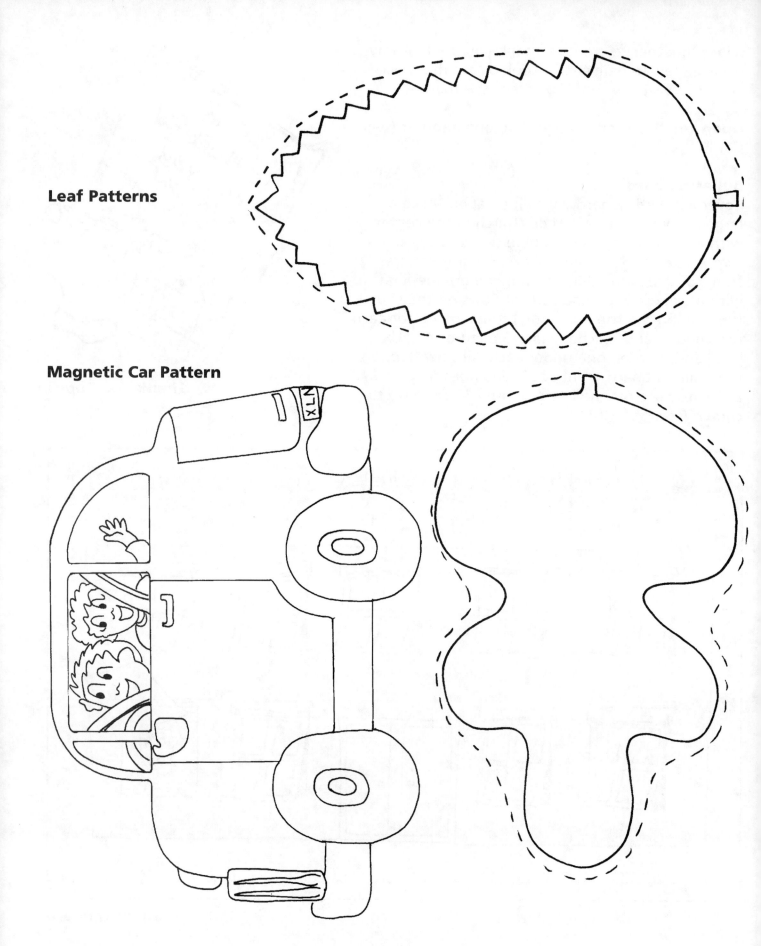

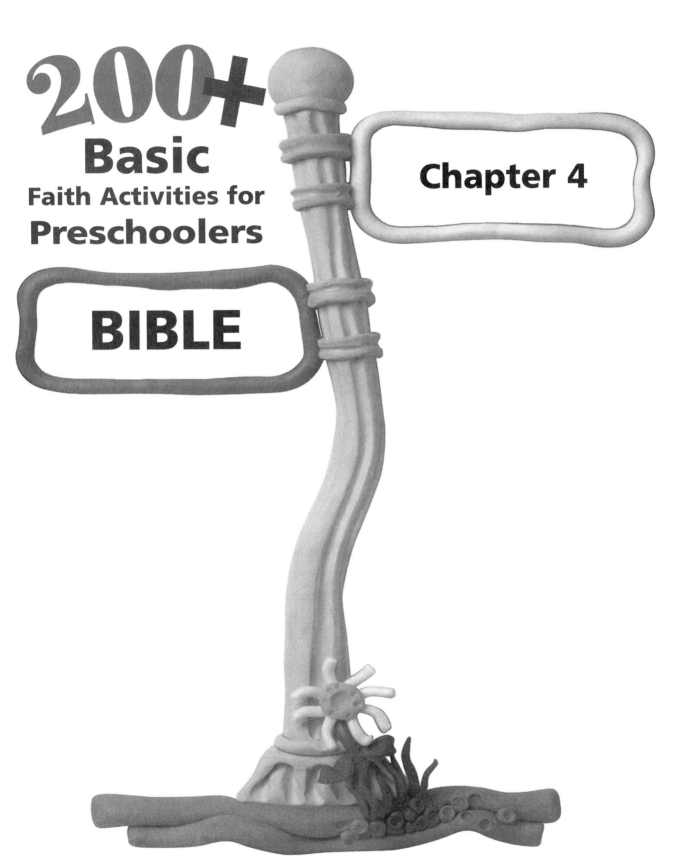

200+ Basic
Faith Activities for Preschoolers

Chapter 4

BIBLE

Rolling Golf Balls

Helping Others Lacy Bookmarks

Bible

Bible-Thought Hide-and-Seek

On brightly colored index cards, print Bible thoughts (one per card), and "hide" in obvious places around the room. Using index cards the same colors as the hidden cards, place these cards at the appropriate references in a Bible.

Encourage preschoolers to look around the room and find one card. When they have found one, lead them to find its matching color in the Bible. Whisper the Bible thought in the preschooler's ear, then encourage her to say it out loud. After everyone has "read" their Bible thought, allow preschoolers to take turns "hiding" the Bible thoughts and finding them again.

Rolling Golf Balls

For threes and older preschoolers, provide a 2-foot length of 3-inch PVC pipe and a basket of golf balls. On each golf ball have a small strip of paper with a Bible thought written on it glued to the ball. Tilt the pipe up for preschoolers, and guide them to place the golf balls down the tube. As the golf ball rolls out, ask: Where did it go?

When the ball is discovered, read the Bible thought on it. Have preschoolers say the Bible thought after you.

Helping Others Lacy Bookmarks

Materials: poster board cut into 2-by-8-inch strips, glue, markers, variety of lace

In advance, cut poster board into strips and lace into 2-inch and 8-inch pieces. On the strips, at the top or bottom, print *All that the Bible says is from God (see 2 Tim. 3:16).*

Guide preschoolers to glue pieces of lace around a strip of poster board. Encourage them to decorate their bookmarks as they wish.

Talk with preschoolers about whom they would like to give their bookmarks. Consider giving them to the elderly or those who are shut-ins in your church.

The Bible Is a Special Book

Along with the regular selection of books, provide a variety of Bibles. Provide as many children's Bibles as possible.

Take time to read and share a Bible with an

interested preschooler. Say: The Bible is a special book. Thank You, God, for the Bible.

Sending Special Messages
Materials: plain paper, postcards, markers, crayons, small chalkboard, chalk, Bible, table, two chairs

Set up a writing center. Guide boys and girls to use the materials to make special messages for their family and friends. Say: The Bible is a special book that tells us about God, Jesus, and the way we are to treat other people. We read in the Bible the words: *Love one another (see 1 John 4:7).* You are showing love when you help someone.
Teaching Tip: Attach a piece of butcher paper to a wall or cover a table. Lead preschoolers to write messages to one another on the paper. Let them share their messages.

Sending Special Messages

Bibles, Bibles
Place a variety of children's Bibles on a table. Place colored index cards at some of the more familiar stories. Prop some open to display pictures. Encourage preschoolers to look at them. Read a familiar Bible story to them.
Open the Bible and read: All that the Bible says is from God (see 2 Tim. 3:16).

Spinning the Bottle
Material: empty 2-liter plastic bottle

Invite the preschoolers to sit in a circle. Place the bottle in the center. Begin by spinning the bottle. When it stops, the child the top points to will say a Bible thought. Take time for all preschoolers to have a turn.

Spinning the Bottle

Nuts and Bolts
Provide a shoe box full of large nuts and bolts for preschoolers to work with. Demonstrate how to turn the nuts on the bolts so that they come off and on. Praise a child for his efforts. Say: The Bible says to work with your hands (see 1 Thess. 4:11). You are doing what the Bible says!

Bible Markers
Display several Bibles in the area. Guide preschoolers to make Bible markers to place in the Bibles. Print the Bible thought below on each marker.
Open the Bible and read: All that the Bible says is from God (see 2 Tim. 3:16).

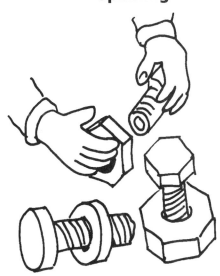

Nuts and Bolts

Everyone Needs a Bible

Make a bed on the floor with a sleeping bag and pillow. Make a nightstand with blocks and put a Bible on top. Talk about hotels. Pretend that the sleeping bag is a hotel bed. Encourage preschoolers to go to bed and read the Bible. Say: Everyone needs a Bible. **Open the Bible and read:** The Bible is useful for teaching us how to live (see 2 Tim. 3:16).

Campfire Bible Study

Materials: stones; small logs; orange construction paper; sleeping bag; Bibles; songbooks; sticks; large marshmallows; allergy alert chart (p. 93)

Post the chart to notify parents of this activity. Lead preschoolers to make a campfire with real stones, small logs, and construction-paper flames. Spread the sleeping bag next to the fire, and pretend to roast marshmallows. Read from a Bible.
Caution: Supervise carefully when using marshmallows and sticks. Advise preschoolers to take small bites and chew carefully.

Bible-Thought Book

Print each Bible thought below on a sheet of colored typing paper. Find a picture that illustrates each thought, and glue it on the matching page. Keep these pages in a three-ring binder, and add future Bible thoughts to the collection.

Share the book with preschoolers. Show preschoolers where Bible thoughts are found in the Bible.
Bible Thoughts:
God made the flowers (see Gen. 1:11).
Everything God made was very good (see Gen. 1:31).
Look at the wonderful things God made (see Job 37:14).
God made the ocean and the dry land (see Psalm 95:5).
The Lord is good (see Psalm 100:3).
God gives food to us (see Psalm 136:25).
We work together (see 1 Cor. 3:9).
God gives us things to enjoy (see 1 Tim. 6:17).

Bible-Thought Book

Starting a Children's Bible Club

Provide Bibles, markers, and paper. Lead preschoolers to make invitations to invite someone to Bible club. Help preschoolers role-play walking door-to-door inviting children to come to Bible club.

Telling Bible Stories
Open a children's Bible to a familiar Bible story, and tell preschoolers the story.
Open the Bible and read: All that the Bible says is from God (see 2 Tim. 3:16).

Bible-Verse Trains
Materials: photocopies of train pattern (p. 42), marker; scissors; Bible

In advance, make photocopies of the train pattern.

Encourage preschoolers to help "hook up" the train. Read the Bible thoughts as you work with preschoolers. Say: Many people ride trains to go to work or to the city.
Teaching Tip: Ask preschoolers to repeat the Bible thought after you read it. Show them where the words are found in the Bible.

Bibles and Books in Many Languages
Materials: picture Bibles or printed materials in a variety of languages, pictures and photographs of a variety of people

Show interested preschoolers the Bibles, books, or other materials. Explain that different people use different languages to talk. Say: God loves all people. People need to know that God loves them, too.
Open the Bible and read: All that the Bible says is from God (see 2 Tim. 3:16).

Helping Refugees
Materials: clothing articles; empty food containers and water bottles; shoes; basic toiletry items (toothbrush, soap, shampoo, etc.), Bible bookmarks or pamphlets; New Testaments

Suggest preschoolers role-play helping refugees. Some can be the workers while others can be refugees. Encourage them to pretend to give the items to the refugees, along with a Bible bookmark, pamphlet, or New Testament. Say: Everyone needs a Bible.
Teaching Tip: Explain the meaning of *refugee* to preschoolers.

Bible Scavenger Hunt
Materials: variety of Bibles with a Bible thought marker placed in each Bible

Bible-Verse Trains

Help one another (see Gal. 5:13).	Jesus went about doing good (see Acts 10:38).	We work together (see 1 Cor. 3:9).	Jesus loves you (see John 15:12).	Pray for one another (see James 5:16).	Be kind to each other (see Eph. 4:32).

Bible Scavenger Hunt

Craft-Stick Bible Thoughts

Accordion Booklets

In advance, hide the Bibles in various locations around the room.

Lead preschoolers to find the hidden Bibles. When each Bible is found, turn to the Bible marker and read the Bible thought.

Open the Bible and read: All that the Bible says is from God (see 2 Tim. 3:16).

Craft-Stick Bible Thoughts

Materials: colored craft sticks, permanent marker, plastic self-sealing bags

In advance, line up colored craft sticks of the same color and write Bible thoughts by writing one word on each stick. Draw a simple shape around the Bible-thought words (across all the sticks) while the sticks are together. Place craft stick puzzles in plastic bags.

Help preschoolers select a plastic bag and put the Bible-thought puzzle together. Read the Bible thought aloud.

Lift-the-Flap Book

In advance, make a book with Bible thoughts printed on each page. Cover one word in each thought with a paper flap.

Ask preschoolers to help you read the book. Allow them to lift the flap. Say: I am glad God gives us the Bible. The Bible is a special book.

Accordion Booklets

Materials: 12-by-18 construction paper, scissors, heart-shaped stickers, Jesus stickers, magazine photos of people, glue

In advance, fold construction paper lengthwise and cut on the fold. Cut one piece for each preschooler. Accordion fold each piece to make four panels. On the bottom of the panels print the following: (1) *God loves us.* (2) *God sent us Jesus.* (3) *Jesus is our friend.* (4) *Jesus said, "Love one another."*

Guide preschoolers to place stickers and pictures on each panel. Say: the Bible tells us about God and His Son, Jesus.

Bulletin Board—Enlistment Idea

Cover the bulletin board with white paper. Display a large Bible cutout in the center of the board. Cut letters from construction paper to read *The Bible Tells Us . . .* Display these words across the top of the bulletin board. Post various Bible thoughts written on different colors of construction paper around the edges of the board. At the bottom of the bulletin board, provide a pocket filled with flyers or cards about classes at your church.

Bulletin Board—Enlistment Idea

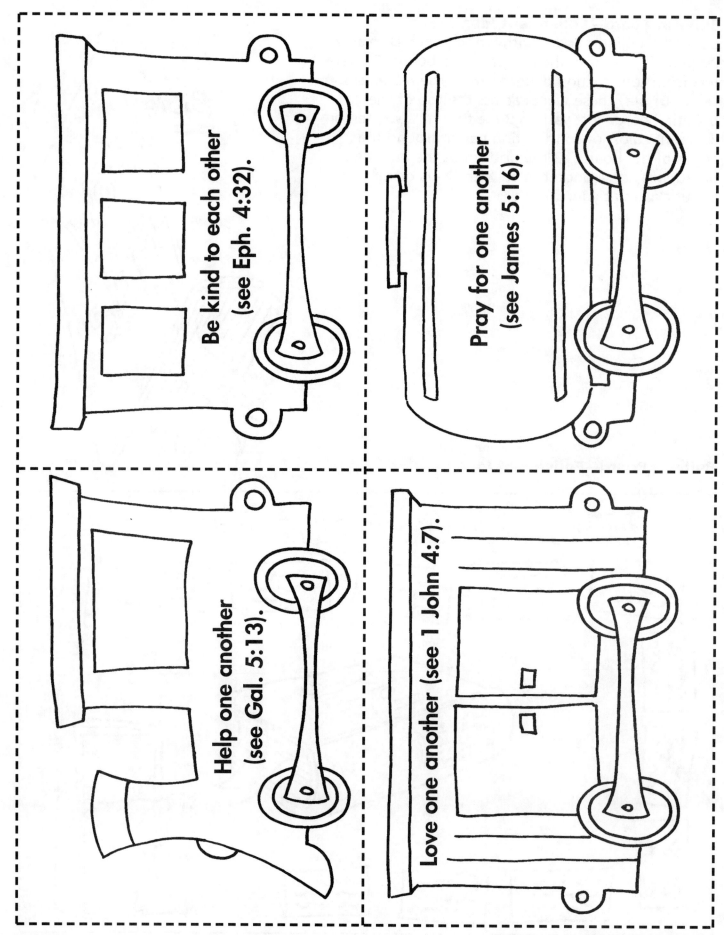

Be kind to each other (see Eph. 4:32).

Pray for one another (see James 5:16).

Help one another (see Gal. 5:13).

Love one another (see 1 John 4:7).

200+ Basic Faith Activities for Preschoolers

200+ Basic
Faith Activities for
Preschoolers

FAMILY

Chapter 5

Family

Families Work Together
Encourage cooperation as preschoolers pretend to make a meal or clean house. Say: How do you help your family? Let's pretend we are a family. What can you do to help?
Open the Bible and read: Help one another (see Gal. 5:13).

Family Montage
Materials: large sheets of construction paper cut into the shape of a heart, pictures of children and adults cut from old magazines, glue

Give each child a construction-paper heart. Lead preschoolers to glue pictures to their hearts to represent their families. Encourage preschoolers to overlap pictures and cover their hearts as much as possible. Talk with preschoolers about their families while they are working. Say: Thank You, God, for families.

Caring for Baby
Materials: sturdy baby dolls, infant bathtub or dishpan, baby towels and washcloths, small diaper bags, baby hairbrush, doll clothes, baby bottles, child-sized rocking chairs

Place a small amount of water in a bathtub, and place with other materials. Encourage preschoolers to bathe, dress, feed, and rock their baby dolls. Say: God gives us families to care for us just like you are caring for your baby. Thank You, God, for families.

God Gave Us All a Family
To the tune of "Have You Ever Seen a Lassie?" sing:
God gave us all a family, a family, a family.
God gave us all a family, to love you and me.
Sing the song a second time but substitute the last phrase with He loves you and me.

Auto Shop
Materials: coveralls, gloves, toolbox, wrench, screwdriver, measuring tape, flashlight, tricycle or wagon to be repaired, cloth for wiping hands

Encourage conversation about taking the family car to the garage for repairs. Say: God wants us to help one another and to love one another.
Open the Bible and read: Help one another (see Gal. 5:13), and Love one another (see 1 John 4:7).

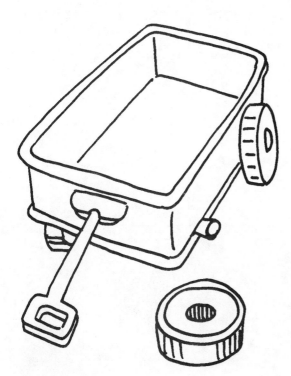

Family Montage

Auto Shop

44

Marble Heart

Materials: large heart shapes cut from construction paper (to fit into cake pans); disposable cake pans; marbles; thin red, pink, and purple paint; cups; spoons; aprons; markers

In advance, print *Love one another (see 1 John 4:7)* on each heart. Put paint in cups, and drop several marbles in each color.

Invite preschoolers to place a heart shape in a cake pan, and spoon marbles (with paint) onto the heart. Show them how to tip the pan, roll marbles around, and let the marbles paint the heart. Say: You can share this with your family.

Marble Heart

Family Journal

Materials: wallpaper or fabric for book covers, plain paper, yarn, parent letter

In advance, send a letter home with the journals, asking families to work with their preschoolers making a family journal. The family decides if they want to journal about a favorite vacation or a favorite activity the family participated in together.

At the end of the month, invite families to come to share their journals with each other.

We Are Different

Materials: photo album, blank white pages to fit into the album, a picture of each child, ink pad, paper towels

In advance, ask parents of each child to send in a family picture. Print on each blank page: *(Child's name) has (color) _____ eyes and (color) _____ hair. _____ (Number of people) people are in his (her) family.*

Guide each child to press his thumb on the ink pad. Then make his thumbprint on the page. Put each child's page in the photo album. Title the album *We Are Different.*

Open the Bible and read: God made people (see Gen. 1:27).

We Are Different

Mother's Day Rock

Materials: smooth, clean rocks; aprons; tempera paint; brushes; glue; acrylic sealer; newspaper; waxed paper; photo of each preschooler; permanent marker

Spread newspaper on a table. After they put on aprons, invite preschoolers to paint a rock. Place wet rocks on waxed paper to dry. When dry, write each

child's name and the date on the bottom of the rock. Trim photos closely around each child. Paint white glue over the area for the photo, and apply the photo. Dry and spray with an acrylic sealer. Suggest preschoolers give the rocks to their moms on Mother's Day or to their dads on Father's Day.
Teaching Tip: Be sensitive to preschoolers who do not have a mom or dad in the home. Suggest other uses for the gift.
Open the Bible and read: Love your father and mother (see Ex. 20:12).

New Moms Ministry—Enlistment Idea
Begin a ministry for new mothers in your church. Ask mothers-to-be for phone numbers and addresses. Give them a card with your name and number, and ask them to call you when the baby arrives.

Before babies are born, make new-baby bags in blue and pink colors. Inside each bag, include several newborn diapers, and some of the following: bib, rattle, pacifier, baby powder, baby shampoo, baby lotion, and so on. Make sure to include something for the new mom, such as a candle or small hand lotion.

When a new mom calls, deliver a new-baby bag to the proud parents. Invite parents to call you if they need help or have a new-baby question. Keep your visit short, but follow up at a later time with friendly phone calls.

New Moms Ministry— Enlistment Idea

Father's Day Pencil Holder
Materials: clean metal cans with duct tape on the edges of the opening, markers, glue, new pencils, construction paper with a shirt drawn on it cut to fit around cans, precut construction-paper-tie shapes

Give each child a can, wrapper, and a tie shape. Show preschoolers how to draw plaid or stripes on the tie shapes. Guide them to glue the ties on the paper shirt. Print *Happy Father's Day, Love(child's name)*. Glue the paper wrapper onto the can. Place a new pencil in the pencil holder. Let preschoolers give the pencil holders to their fathers.
Note: Be sensitive to any preschoolers who may not have a father.

Father's Day Pencil Holder

Family Quilt
In advance, call the preschoolers' parents and ask them to send in a family photograph.

Arrange photographs on a quilt. Include one of your own. Read the pictures together. Say: Families are important.

Open the Bible and read: Jesus' family went to church (see Luke 2:27).

Handprint Kites
Materials: newspaper, scissors, yarn, paint, pie pans, apron, short fabric strips, tape

In advance, prepare newspaper by cutting sheets into large diamonds. Layer several together and staple the edges closed. Make enough for each preschooler to have one.

Invite preschoolers to decorate a kite with painted handprints. While the paint dries, help them tie fabric strips onto a piece of yarn for the tail. Attach the yarn to the kite with tape. Print *Pray for families.* along one side.

Handprint Kites

Helping Others Sharing Bread
Invite preschoolers and their families to donate a loaf of bread to be delivered to a local food bank or homeless shelter. Lead preschoolers to help make Bible bookmarks shaped like a loaf of bread. On the bookmark print, *God cares for you (see 1 Peter 5:7).* Attach one of these bookmarks to each loaf of bread. If possible, invite preschoolers to participate in the delivery of the bread and bookmarks. Say: God wants families to help others.

Snowball Cookies
Materials: 2 cups flour, 1 teaspoon milk, ⅔ cup oil, 4 or 5 tablespoons water, powdered sugar, mixing bowl, cookie sheet, oven

As a family make these cookies. Lead preschoolers to help you place the first four ingredients in a bowl. Mix with hands or forks. Guide preschoolers to roll the dough into small balls. Bake on a greased cookie sheet at 325°F for 10 minutes. Cool. Sprinkle with powdered sugar. Enjoy your snowball cookies as you thank God for each member of your family.

Families
Materials: small photo album, instant-picture camera, permanent marker

In advance, call your preschoolers' parents, and ask them to bring a photograph of the family to class.

Helping Others Sharing Bread

Families Cube

Use the camera to take a photograph of each child. Place the photographs in a small photo album. Label the photo pages. As preschoolers look at the photo album, say: God planned for families.

Families Cube
Materials: construction paper, glue, scissors, old magazines

Make a paper cube. Lead preschoolers to locate and cut pictures of families or people from magazines. Glue the pictures on the cube to make a collage on each of the six sides.

Invite preschoolers to roll the cube and help tell a story about the people on the face of the cube facing upwards. Say: Families are very important. I'm glad God gives us families.
Open the Bible and read: Love your father and mother (see Ex. 20:12).

Helping Others Preschool Treat Bags
Materials: gallon-sized, self-sealing plastic bags; small toys; crayons; pencils; notepads, toiletries; fabric; ribbon

Invite families of preschoolers to come and work together to pack bags with age-appropriate books, crayons, toiletries, etc., for young children. Wrap the bags in colorful fabric tied with ribbon. Attach a card signed by preschoolers. Take the gift bags to a children's shelter, children's hospital, or other appropriate agency.

**Helping Others
Preschool Treat Bags**

200+ Basic Faith Activities for Preschoolers

SELF

Chapter 6

Self

Watch the Hands
Invite preschoolers to play a "no words" game. Lead them to make their hands do the same action that you do. Remind them it is a quiet, shh, no-talking game. Lead in the following hand movements:

Clap your hands.
Shake your hands.
Put your hands on your head.
Put your hands behind you.
Clap your hands above your head, then below your waist.

Continue the game as long as preschoolers are interested. Give the boys and girls an opportunity to be the leader and talk with their hands. Say: Look what you can do!

How Would I Look?
Place several colors of dry-erase markers near a full-length mirror. As preschoolers look in the mirror, lead them to draw different features or costumes on their reflections. Say: How would you look with blue hair?

Then lead them to draw themselves with blue hair. When finished, always remind preschoolers you are glad God made them just the way they are. Be sure to use paper towels or tissues to erase the mirror drawings.

Open the Bible and read: God made me (see Psalm 139:14).

God Made Me Books
In advance, print *God Made Me* on folded sheets of light colors of construction paper to make a book cover for each preschooler. Fold a sheet of copier or typing paper in half and tuck into the cover to resemble a book. Punch three holes down the folded side and tie the papers together with lengths of yarn.

Encourage preschoolers to color the covers of their books. Lead them to draw pictures of what they like about themselves in the book. Say: God made you.

Dusty Art
Materials: disposable pie tins, large cotton balls, sidewalk chalk, construction paper

In advance, fill cotton balls with chalk dust by rubbing them along the side of the sidewalk chalk. Place a different color of chalk dust cotton in each pie tin.

Watch the Hands

God Made Me Books

50

Give each preschooler a piece of construction paper. Lead them to choose a cotton ball and dab it on their papers. Encourage them to smear the colors together to make different designs. Say: Thank You, God, for eyes to see.

Fragrant Art
In advance, gather fruit-scented markers (grape, orange, cherry, etc.).

Provide large sheets of construction paper. Talk to preschoolers about the fruity fragrances of the markers. As they draw on their papers, say: Thank You, God, for noses to smell.

Caution: Do not allow preschoolers to sniff the markers.

Cookie-Cutter Match
On a half sheet of poster board, trace the outline of several different shaped cookie cutters. Place cookie cutters in a plastic bowl, and then place in the area with the poster board. Guide preschoolers to match the cookie cutters with the outlines on the board.

Cookie-Cutter Match

I Am Special!
Materials: photo of each child, scales, tape measure, crayons, stapler, staples, construction paper, scissors

In advance, collect a photograph of each preschooler or take photographs with an instant-picture camera. Fold construction paper in half to make a booklet for each child. Make a cutout on the front cover so that the photograph shows through underneath the title *I Am Special.*

Help preschoolers complete the book with important information, such as how much they weigh, how tall they are, and what they can do.

Open the Bible and read: I am wonderfully made (see Psalm 139:14).

Terrific Tubes
In advance, collect cardboard tubes from gift wrap, kitchen wrap, toilet tissue, etc. Paint them with tempera paint, then coat them with a nontoxic clear finish.

Guide preschoolers to arrange the tubes in artistic designs, count them, or sort them by color and size. Discuss how the tubes are alike and different. and how preschoolers are alike and different. Say: Thank You, God, for making Jordan just the way she is.

Open the Bible and read: God made us (see Psalm 100:3).

I Am Special!

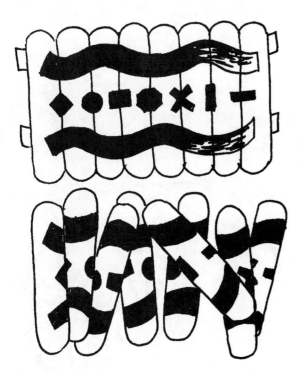

Puzzle Sticks

Puzzle Sticks

Materials: 8 tongue depressors (for each puzzle), colored permanent markers, masking tape, self-sealing sandwich bags

In advance, use two strips of tape on the back of tongue depressors to hold them together while you work. On the top side, draw a design with a pencil, then fill it in with the permanent markers. Part of the design must be on each stick. Remove the tape strips. Place in a bag.

Place puzzles on the floor. Encourage preschoolers to line up depressors side by side to complete a puzzle. Praise their efforts.

Magnetic Puzzles

Materials: pictures of camels and sheep, poster board, self-adhesive magnetic tape, steel cookie sheets

In advance, glue pictures of camels and sheep onto poster board then cut into large puzzle pieces. Cut small strips of magnetic tape and attach to the back of each puzzle piece.

Place puzzle pieces and cookie sheets on a table, and guide preschoolers to put the puzzles together on the cookie sheets. Say: I see you working with your hands. The Bible says, Work with your hands (see 1 Thess. 4:11). You are doing what the Bible says!

Round Things

Round Things

Cut a 6-inch circle in the side of a cardboard box. Challenge preschoolers to find round or circular objects in the classroom that will fit through the hole. For younger preschoolers, provide a basket of round items to drop into the hole. For older preschoolers, prepare a box for square and triangular items, and have them look for three different shapes of objects. Say: You are growing. You can do many things.

Hands on Shoulders

Share the following action rhyme with preschoolers:
Hands on shoulders, hands on knees,
Hands behind you, if you please;
Touch your shoulders, now your nose,
Now your hair, and now your toes.
Hands up high in the air,
Down at your sides; now touch your hair;
Hands up high as before,
Now clap your hands, one, two, three, four.

Follow the Leader

Provide lively instrumental music for this activity.

Lead preschoolers in a follow-the-leader game around the room as you walk, run, gallop, etc.

Invite preschoolers to join you in doing various movements while standing in place. For example, you might tap a steady beat on the head, shoulders, and knees; reach up with one hand and then the other; move your elbows up and down; twist from side to side, etc.

Say: Look at you. You can do many things. Thank You, God, that (call child's name) is growing, and that he can do many things all by himself.

Simple Drums

Materials: whipped topping bowls with lids, plastic or metal bowls, various sizes of pots and pans, wooden spoons

Place whipped topping bowls with lids on the floor. Turn other bowls and pots and pans upside down and place them in the area.

Encourage younger preschoolers to use the wooden spoons to "play" the drums. Praise preschoolers for the music they make. Say: Thank You, God, for hands to play the drums.

Handprints

Materials: unbreakable mirror, hand lotion

Drop a small amount of lotion in a preschooler's hand. Guide him to put his hand flat against the mirror, then lift it up. Admire his handiwork. Say: The Bible says, God made you. Thank You, God, for (child's name).
Open the Bible and read: God made me (see Psalm 139:14).

Milk-Jug Ball Game

In advance, make a jug bucket from an empty plastic milk jug by cutting away the top section with scissors (leaving the handle). Place duct tape over the edges. Place several tennis balls in the jug and set on the floor.

Let younger preschoolers discover the milk jug and balls. Watch as they dump the jug, or reach in and grab the balls. Help gather balls, and let preschoolers put the balls back in the jug. Say: You can do many things.

Remember Where

Materials: red, green, and blue (or any three different colors) plastic disposable cups; golf ball; small toy; small artificial flower

Simple Drums

Milk-Jug Ball Game

All Do This

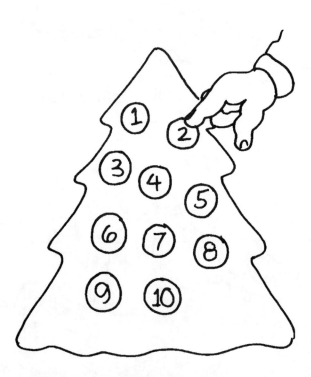

Count the Ornaments

Turn cups upside down and place the golf ball, toy, and flower under each one. When a preschooler comes to the area, lift up each cup and show what is underneath. Next move the cups around, and ask: Where is the ball? Where is the toy? Where is the flower?

When a preschooler answers, lift up the cup to see if he is correct. Be sure to praise each preschooler's efforts.

What's That Sound?
In advance, record familiar sounds to a preschooler (car horn, dog barking, door shutting, your own voice, bell ringing, etc.).

Play the recording for preschoolers. Pause the recording after each sound and guide preschoolers to identify each sound. Say: Thank You, God, for ears to hear.

All Do This
Suggest preschoolers stand in a circle. One child is in the center. Chant or sing:
Adam had seven sons, Seven sons had Adam.
The seven sons were happy and glad.
And they all did as Adam bade.
"All do what I do," said Adam.
On the last line, the players in the circle watch the actions of the person in the middle. They then copy his actions. The person in the middle calls on someone to take his place in the middle. Say: Look what you can do.
Teaching Tip: Use the name of the child who is in the middle.

Count the Ornaments
Materials: green, yellow, red, and blue felt; scissors; marker
In advance, cut one tree out of the green felt and cut ten ornaments using the yellow, red, and blue felt. Number the ornaments one through ten.

Suggest preschoolers work together or take turns placing the ornaments on the tree. Ask the older preschoolers to put the ornaments on the tree in the correct counting order.

Place Mat Puzzles
Use inexpensive vinyl place mats to make simple preschool puzzles. Using cookie cutters trace no more than four or five designs onto a place mat. Cut out designs with a utility knife.

Separate designs from the place mats and place in a basket. Lead preschoolers to place the cutouts in the place mats where they belong.

54

Say: You are a helper. The Bible tells us to Help one another (see Gal. 5:13).

When the Music Stops, Play Ball

In advance, cut out baseballs from construction paper, having the same number balls as preschoolers in the room. Print a numeral on each ball.

Place the baseballs on the floor in a circle. Ask the preschoolers to stand in front of a baseball. Play a short part of a CD or tape as the preschoolers move around the circle. When the music stops, each child picks up the ball he is standing by. Call on a child and give instructions for him to do an action the same number of times as the numeral on the baseball he is holding. For example, say to Nick: You have the numeral two on your baseball. Jump up and down two times. Say: Look what you can do.

Continue the game, giving different instructions for the preschoolers to do.

Bells for Babies

Securely sew small jingle bells to 4-inch lengths of elastic. Sew ends together and place around the ankles or wrist of babies. Babies will be fascinated by the sound as they kick their legs and move their arms about. Say: Thank You, God, for ears to hear.

Surprise Drawing

Materials: box with a lid, paper, scissors, crayons

In advance, cut a hole in the box large enough for a child to put her hand inside. Cut the paper to fit the bottom of the box.

Put the lid on the box. Invite the child to try a fun way to make a picture. Guide her to draw a picture on the paper inside the box without looking at what she is drawing. Help her remove the paper revealing her surprise drawing. Say: God made you. You are very special.

Brag Books

Purchase several brag books (small photo albums). Choose a theme, such as jungle or green things. Find and cut out pictures from magazines, greeting cards, and junk mail. Place in the brag book. "Read" the pictures with preschoolers. Say: You can do many things.
Teaching Tip: Take pictures of preschoolers as they play. Keep pictures in a brag book.

Flowerpot Blocks

For younger preschoolers, provide plastic flowerpots of

When the Music Stops, Play Ball

Surprise Drawing

various sizes for stacking and nesting. Demonstrate stacking the flowerpots to build a wall. Encourage preschoolers to help you. Praise their efforts. Say: You are such a good helper. Thank you for your help.

Self Portraits

Materials: construction paper, watercolor paints and brushes, aprons, mirror, scissors, glue

Ask preschoolers to look in the mirror, and then lead them to paint a picture of themselves with watercolors. When dry, trim around each portrait, and glue to a sheet of black construction paper. Display. Say: Look at how different we are. God made each of us special.

Reading House

In advance, turn a large appliance box into a reading house by cutting out a door and two windows. Remove the top, and attach a battery powered clip-on light. Use fabric scraps and hot glue to make curtains. Place pillows on the floor and a rug at the door. Print *Reading House* over the door, and arrange books that focus on the Christian concept of self inside on the floor.

Invite preschoolers to read in the reading house.

The Name Game

Materials: tagboard, envelopes, black marker, scissors, envelopes

In advance, print each child's name on two separate pieces of tagboard. Cut the letters apart on one of the name cards. Put the cut letters and the name card in an envelope on which the child's name is printed.

When a child shows interest, give her the envelope with her name. Lay the name card on the table in front of her. Next, ask her to shake up the letters in the envelope and spill them out on the table. Then she can match the cutout letters to the letters in her name. Say: God loves you. You are special.

Ten Little Fingers

Read this poem to preschoolers. Lead them to create their own movement picture, using different movements to illustrate the actions the poem mentions.

Ten Little Fingers

I have ten little fingers
And they all belong to me.
I can make them do things.
Would you like to see?
I can shut them up tight

Reading House

The Name Game

56

Or open them wide.
I can put them together
Or make them all hide.
I can make them jump high,
I can make them jump low.
I can fold them quietly
And say a prayer, just so.

Book of Names
Take and develop a picture of each preschooler. Place each picture on a piece of construction paper. Print each child's name under his picture. Bind along the left side by punching holes and using metal rings.

Help preschoolers read names. Older preschoolers can have fun copying each other's names and talking about the letters.

Book of Names

Are You Listening?
Materials: 6, 35 mm film canisters; self-adhesive color dots; uncooked popcorn; sand; water

In advance, fill pairs of canisters with popcorn, sand, and water. Tape on lids securely. Color code each pair for checking with dots on the bottoms.

Guide preschoolers to pair the canisters by gently shaking and listening to the contents of each. Show them how to check their work by looking at the bottoms. Say: Thank You, God, for ears to hear.

Make a Kazoo
Materials: tissue tubes, waxed paper cut into 4-inch squares, markers, masking tape

Suggest each preschooler decorate his tube with markers. Show how to lay a piece of waxed paper on the table and place the tube standing up on the center. Tape two opposing corners to the tube with tape. Demonstrate how to blow and hum into the opposite end of the kazoo to make music. Say: You can play the kazoo. God made you to do many things.

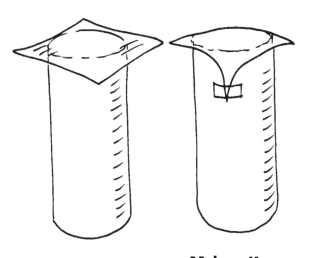

Make a Kazoo

A Matching Game
Materials: wallpaper samples, poster board, glue, scissors

In advance, choose wallpaper samples with bold patterns and colors. Cut poster board into 2-inch squares. Cut two sets of wallpaper into squares. Glue them onto the poster-board squares.

Place the squares facedown on a table or carpeted area. Lead preschoolers to take turns turning over two cards and matching the patterns. Say: The colors and pat-

You Are Special

Cotton

aluminum foil

rd board

Texture Book

terns on these two cards are alike. No one else is exactly like you. God made you special.

Open the Bible and read: I am wonderfully made (see Psalm 139:14).

You Are Special

In advance, ask preschoolers' parents and families to provide several photos of the preschoolers and their families. Insert each photo into a self-sealing plastic bag. Stack the bags together. Print several Bible thoughts on individual pieces of paper and insert into a self-sealing plastic bag. Make a construction-paper cover. Staple the bags together to create a book. Periodically, change the photographs or Bible thoughts.

Read the book with interested preschoolers. Say: God made you. You are special.

Texture Book

Materials: velvet, sandpaper, aluminum foil, cotton, corrugated cardboard, other interesting textures, construction paper, hole punch, large binder rings

In advance, make a texture book with one of the fabrics or materials mounted on each page. Bind the book together with the rings.

Invite interested preschoolers to explore the book with you. Challenge them to describe how each texture feels. Can they name the fabric or material on each page? Can they think of objects made from that fabric or material?

200+ Basic Faith Activities for Preschoolers

COMMUNITY

Chapter 7

Community

Helping the Sick
Materials: dolls; doll beds; pillows and sheets; empty, cleaned medicine bottles; child's doctor kit; Bible

Lead preschoolers to arrange an area to look like a hospital. Guide them to role-play taking care of the dolls. Encourage preschoolers to think of ways they could help someone who was sick.

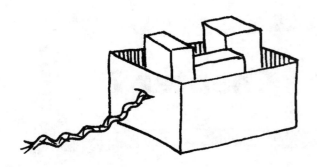

Pull Toy

Pull Toy
For younger preschoolers, make a pull toy by attaching a rope to a small box. Lead preschoolers to load the box with blocks and pull it around the room. Encourage preschoolers to work together to load the box. Say: The Bible says, Help one another (see Gal. 5:13). Thank you for helping.

Who Is My Friend?
As you sit in a circle with preschoolers, describe something about one of the preschoolers while the others try to guess who it is. Say: My friend is wearing tennis shoes. Who is my friend?

If they do not say who you are describing, give another clue. Say: My friend is wearing a red ribbon. Who is my friend?
Open the Bible and read: A friend loves at all times (see Prov. 17:17).

Making a City Play Area
Materials: white, twin-sized, flat sheet; fabric tube paint; assorted boxes covered with construction paper; small toy vehicles and airplanes

In advance, using fabric paints, draw roads, a park, an airport, and city blocks on the sheet Draw windows and doors onto the box "buildings." Leave the city blocks blank so that preschoolers can add the buildings. Make the roads the width of a 3- or 4-inch car or truck.

Spread the sheet on the floor. Encourage preschoolers to add the buildings and to play with the vehicles. Say: Some people live in big cities. Where do you live?

Making a City Play Area

Air Ball
Materials: full-sized flat sheet, soft foam basketball

60

Spread the sheet on the floor. Lead preschoolers to stand around the sheet and pick up the edges. Place the ball in the middle of the sheet. Instruct preschoolers to hold on tightly as they make the ball go up in the air by waving the sheet up and down, then catch the ball in the sheet.

The object of this activity is to get the ball in the air and to make sure it always lands inside the sheet. Say: You are working together to keep the ball in the air.

Prayer Pockets
Materials: two paper plates for each preschooler; stapler; hole punch; 8-inch lengths of yarn; colored index cards, seven per child; crayons

In advance, to make each pocket, cut one of the paper plates in half. Invert the paper plate half and staple it to the whole paper plate. Print at the bottom of each half *I will pray.*

Give each preschooler seven index cards. Assist them in printing on each card the name of someone they can pray for. Lead preschoolers to decorate their prayer pockets and place the cards in the pockets. Punch a hole in the top of each pocket and thread a length of yarn through the hole.

Encourage preschoolers to hang their pockets at home and take out a card each day and pray for that person.

Prayer Pockets

Helping Others Plant for Someone III
Materials: several small flowering bedding plants, potting soil, large plastic flower pot, small garden shovels or large spoons, watering can

Help preschoolers decide on a person who will receive the plant. This could be someone on the church staff, a preschooler's relative, or a resident in a nearby retirement home.

Guide preschoolers to use spoons or shovels to scoop potting soil into the flowerpot. Carefully remove plants from their cartons and assist preschoolers in placing them in the flowerpot. Attach a note to each flowerpot that reads *Love each other (see John 15:17).*

**Helping Others
Plant for Someone III**

City or Country?
Cut pictures from old magazines representing things found in the city and things found in the country. Glue each picture to a large index card.

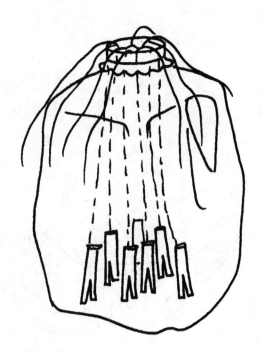

Solving Problems

Place cards in an area along with a basket and a stainless steel bowl. Guide preschoolers to look at cards and place the city cards in the bowl and the country cards in the basket. Encourage conversation about each picture.

Solving Problems

Help older preschoolers learn to work cooperatively. Provide a plastic milk jug with a narrow opening, several peg-type clothespins, and string. Tie a piece of string to each clothespin, and then place them in the milk jug, leaving the strings hanging out of the jug. Ask the preschoolers to pull out the strings. Talk to them about what happens (it will be hard to remove them all at one time). Then ask: How can you work together to get the clothespins out?

Say: Yes, taking turns getting out the clothespins is good. Working together is good. Thank you for working together. People in our community work together. Working together makes Jesus happy.
Open the Bible and read: We work together (see 1 Cor. 3:9).

Helping Others Making Peanut Butter Balls

1 cup peanut butter
1 cup instant dry milk
2 tablespoons honey
chopped nuts or granola

Post the allergy alert chart (p. 93) for peanuts.

Mix peanut butter and dry milk. Stir in honey a little at a time. Form into balls the size of walnuts. Roll in chopped nuts or granola. Store in airtight container. Makes about 30 balls.

Guide preschoolers to mix and roll balls. Encourage them to think of someone to receive the cookies.

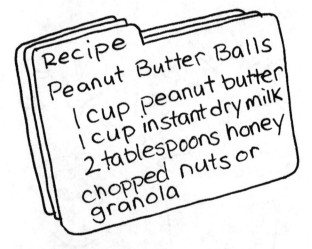

Helping Others Making Peanut Butter Balls

Doctor's Office

Materials: white shirt, plastic gloves, eye chart, cot, stethoscope, bandages, pencil, paper, clipboard, baby doll

Talk to the preschoolers about their visits to the doctor. Say: Doctors and nurses are community helpers who help people stay healthy.

Lead preschoolers to role-play being doctors and nurses helping others.
Open the Bible and read: Help one another (see Gal. 5:13).

Helping Others Food for Hungry People

Materials: dried beans, rice, small grocery bags, crayons or colored markers

In advance, send home a note asking parents of preschoolers to bring bags of beans and rice to class.

Lead preschoolers to decorate the grocery bags. Put a bag each of beans and rice in each sack. Print the Bible thought, *Love one another (see John 15:17)* on a strip of paper and place one in each bag.

If possible, take preschoolers with you to deliver to a Soup Kitchen or homeless shelter in your area.

Open the Bible and read: Help one another (see Gal. 5:13), and Love one another (see John 15:17).

Making Cookies

Help preschoolers make fish-shaped cookies to give to someone who is ill or shut in. Attach the Bible thought, *God cares for you (see 1 Peter 5:7).*

Place the cookies in a decorated box, and take preschoolers with you to make the delivery.

Open the Bible and read: Help one another (see Gal. 5:13).

Bed and Breakfast

Materials: table, tablecloth, napkins, flowers in a plastic vase, plastic dishes, utensils, paper, pencil

In advance, make a guest book with blank pages for each child to write his name.

Talk about what a bed and breakfast is and ask if anyone's family has stayed in a home that was like a hotel. Guide preschoolers to take turns being the host and hostess for the Bed and Breakfast. The other friends can be the guests who are served breakfast. Remember to get the guests to sign the guest book. Say: Thank You, God, for friends.

Extra: Guide boys and girls to make pancakes or toast to serve the guests for breakfast. Post the allergy alert chart, page 93.

Feeding the Hungry

Place toy food items, plates, utensils, and a Bible on a table. Encourage preschoolers to pretend to be hungry and ask the helper for food. Remind them to take turns role-playing the hungry person and the helper.

**Helping Others
Food for Hungry People**

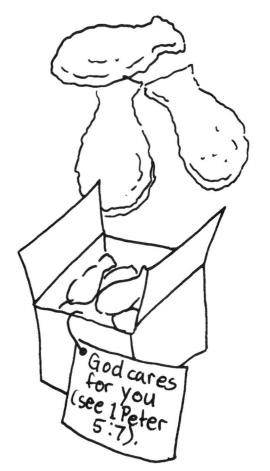

Making Cookies

"I Am Special" Booklets

"I Am Special" Booklets

Materials: construction paper, copier paper, doll and gown patterns on page 70, crayons, yarn, happy-face stickers, plastic sandwich bags, fabric scraps, hook-and-loop fastener, adhesive bandages, stapler

In advance, check with the children's wing of a hospital for permission to put the booklets in the children's playroom. Make four copies of the dolls, and a book cover from construction paper for each booklet. Title the booklet *I Am Special.* Use the gown pattern to cut fabric in gown shapes. Put one side of hook-and-loop fastener on a doll and the other on the gown shape.

Make copies of the pages to go into the booklet: On each page print a sentence of instruction for the child. Page l: *God made me and I am special. This is a picture of me. I can put on my gown.* Page 2: *This is a picture of me. I can draw my favorite toys.* Page 3: *This is a picture of me in the hospital. I can put the band-aid where I hurt.* Page 4: *This is my happy face! Thank You, God, for making me.*

Guide preschoolers to work together putting the items for the booklet into the sandwich bags: one gown piece, one crayon, one bandage, one happy-face sticker. Staple the plastic bag of items to the inside back cover of the booklet. Say: Thank you for helping make the booklets for the children's play-room at the hospital.

Teaching Tip: Invite families to be involved in gathering the materials, putting fasteners on the doll patterns and fabric pieces, and delivering the book-lets.

Community Play Mat

Cover a table with white butcher paper. Working with preschoolers, use markers to draw your community. Make square and rectangle shapes for stores, banks, schools, hospitals, churches, and post office. Add roads, a park, mailboxes, and anything else that preschoolers remember seeing in their community. When complete, give preschoolers toy people and cars.

Open the Bible and read: Help one another (see Gal. 5:13).

Flower Arrangement

Materials: variety of containers such as empty cans with smooth edges or milk cartons (one for each

Community Play Mat

200+ Basic Faith Activities for Preschoolers

child), wrapping paper, shapes cut from wallpaper scraps, flower patterns, crayons, glue

In advance, enlarge, photocopy, and cut out the flowers at right. (Be sure to make enough so each child can have several.)

Invite the boys and girls to choose a container to cover with wrapping paper, and then decorate with the wallpaper shapes. Guide boys and girls to color their flowers and arrange them in their vases.

Suggest that the boys and girls share their vases of flowers with someone special.

Open the Bible and read: Love one another (see 1 John 4:7).

Signs That Help

Materials: poster board, markers, clear self-adhesive plastic, toy vehicles

In advance, draw the following signs on the poster board: *Hospital, Handicapped, Bike Route, Pedestrian Crossing.* Cut out shapes of signs, then cover with self-adhesive plastic.

Show the signs to the preschoolers. Talk about what each sign means and why we have them. Let them show how to use the signs as they build with the blocks.

Time for School

Materials: props for school-related play (paper, folders, pencils, tablets, calculators, etc.)

Lead preschoolers to pretend they are in school. Encourage one preschooler to play the role of teacher. Say: We have schools in our community. Let's pray for teachers and students in our schools.

Canned Food Collection

Invite preschoolers and their parents to help gather canned foods and nonperishable foods to donate to a food shelter or pantry in the church or local community. Say: We are helping feed hungry people in our neighborhood. We can show them we care.

You might want to invite preschoolers to help you decorate a card(s) to take to the pantry or shelter to distribute with the food items.

Gift Holder

Materials: play dough (p. 22); nature items such as sticks, small pinecones, rocks; disposable pie plate; flowers; clear plastic cup; ribbon

Flower Arrangement

Signs That Help

Gift Holder

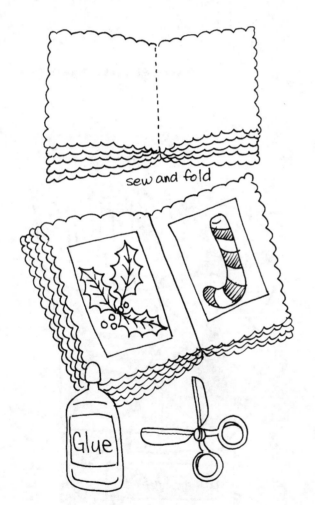

sew and fold

Glue

Greeting-Card Books

In advance, choose someone to receive a gift holder made by the preschoolers. Purchase small flowers or pick some from your garden.

Lead each child to place a small ball of play dough in the pie plate and press it down, filling the plate. Put a plastic cup in the center of the plate. Preschoolers take turns pushing the nature items into the play dough, filling in around the cup. Tie a ribbon around the cup. Lead preschoolers to put flowers inside the holder. Take preschoolers to deliver the gift.

Open the Bible and read: Help one another (see Gal. 5:13).

Greeting-Card Books
Materials: paper place mats, sewing machine, used greeting cards, glue sticks, scissors

In advance, stack five place mats together on top of each other, and sew down the center, forming a book. Make several of these.

Guide preschoolers to select greeting cards, cut off the back half, and glue the front to book pages, one on each page. Fold the place mats along the sewing line, forming a book. Donate to a homeless shelter.

Cleanup Walk
Take preschoolers on a cleanup walk. **In advance,** post the allergy alert chart (p. 93), and advise parents that preschoolers will be going to a nearby park or the church grounds to pick up trash. Instruct preschoolers to gather safe trash, such as cans, paper, and plastic. Tell them that you will pick up unsafe garbage, like broken glass, food items, bottles, or sharp items. Give each child a plastic garbage bag and rubber gloves, and go for your walk.

Place all trash in a garbage can. Wash hands when you are done collecting garbage. Say: We are helping our neighborhood to look nice. Thank you for helping.

Heart Find
Cut 15 heart shapes from paper. Print one letter on each shape to spell *Love one another (see 1 John 4:7)*. Hide them in your classroom. Ask preschoolers to find the hearts and put together the message. Read together.

66

Open the Bible and read: Love one another (see 1 John 4:7).

Bible Club Supplies
Materials: brown paper grocery bags, markers and crayons, stickers

In advance, send a note home with preschoolers requesting that they bring needed items for a local after-school Bible club or children's class.

Invite preschoolers to decorate the bags that will be used to carry the donated items. Provide a variety of art materials, including markers, crayons, and stickers from which preschoolers can choose.

Teaching Tip: If possible, take preschoolers with you to deliver the collected items one afternoon after school while the Bible club is meeting.

Heart Find

Community Helpers Puzzles
Materials: pictures of community helpers (firefighter, doctor, teacher, police officer) cut from old magazines; small brown paper bags

In advance, glue each picture to a piece of sturdy cardboard. Laminate, and then cut each picture into three or four pieces. Place each community helper puzzle in a separate paper bag.

As preschoolers put a puzzle together, remind them that they can be a helper at home and in their neighborhood. Help them identify the community helpers and how each one helps others.

Open the Bible and read: We are helpers (see 2 Cor. 1:24).

Paper-Sack Houses
Guide preschoolers to make paper-sack houses with lunch sacks. Draw a door and windows on sacks. Lead preschoolers to open the sacks, and lightly stuff with crumpled newspaper. Fold the top edge down and staple closed. Add a construction-paper roof. Say: Let's pray for everyone to have a home.

Paper-Sack Houses

Helping Hands
Materials: construction paper, crayons and markers, stapler, staples

Lead each child to trace his hand onto a piece of construction paper. Suggest that preschoolers draw a picture of themselves helping someone on or around their hand pattern. Sing to the tune of "Here We Go Round the Mulberry Bush":

Helping Hands

Gifts of Love

This is a way that I can help, I can help, I can help.
This is a way that I can help to show God's love.
Ask each child to tell you about his or her drawing. Write the words the preschooler tells you at the bottom of his hand pattern. Stack the hands and staple along the left side to make a booklet. Look through the helping-hands booklet with preschoolers.

Gifts of Love
Materials: small gift bags or cookie tins; ribbon; commercial cookie dough; plastic knives; cookie sheets; oven; sprinkles; ready-made icing (red, pink, white)

In advance, enlist parents of preschoolers to help donate the gift bags or cookie tins.

Lead preschoolers to help you make sugar cookies. Suggest preschoolers slice cookies using prepared cookie dough. Guide them to place the cookies on a cookie sheet and bake according to package directions. When cookies cool, lead preschoolers to decorate them using the icing and sprinkles. Place several cookies in a gift bag or cookie tin. Encourage preschoolers to make a note to attach to each gift bag. Help preschoolers print *God loves you and so do we!* on each card. Deliver these "gifts of love" to members of your church who are shut-ins or to families or individuals who visit your church.

Hot Chocolate Mix
Materials: individual packages of hot chocolate mix, foam cups, plastic spoons, self-sealing quart-sized bags, Bible bookmark or card with a printed Bible thought

Lead preschoolers to place a package of hot chocolate mix, a cup, a spoon, and a Bible bookmark in each bag. Deliver the bags to a homeless shelter or local food pantry.
Caution: If preschoolers go with you to make the delivery, make sure proper arrangements are made with parents and that enough supervision is available.

Community Helpers Dramatic Play
Materials: dress-up clothes and props, particularly ones that represent the medical field (stethoscopes, white lab coats, nurses' hats, empty prescription bottles); baby dolls

Lead preschoolers to pretend they are nurses and doctors and others who might work in a hospital. Help them care for the babies and other preschoolers who pretend to be patients.

Guess What's in the Bag
Fill a doctor's medical bag with tools or items that a doctor might use (cotton balls, tongue depressor, stethoscope, thermometer, bandages). Invite preschoolers to reach into the bag and feel an object. Ask them to guess what the object is before pulling it from the bag. Direct preschoolers to take turns pulling the objects from the bag. Name each object. Place all the objects in the bag and play again! As preschoolers play, say: Doctors help us feel better when we are sick. Let's thank God for doctors who live in our community.

Guess What's in the Bag

Tray Favors
Lead preschoolers to collect small toiletry items to take to the local nursing home or assisted living facility. Help preschoolers make simple tray favors that can be placed on the residents' trays when meals are served. Create an artificial spring flower for a tray favor. Invert a small disposable cup, and cut a hole through the bottom. Insert a craft stick (to represent a stem). Attach a green construction-paper leaf to the craft stick. Print *God loves us (see 1 John 4:10)* on the leaf. Use cupcake liners and construction paper to make a blossom. Attach the blossom to the top of the craft stick.

Tray Favors

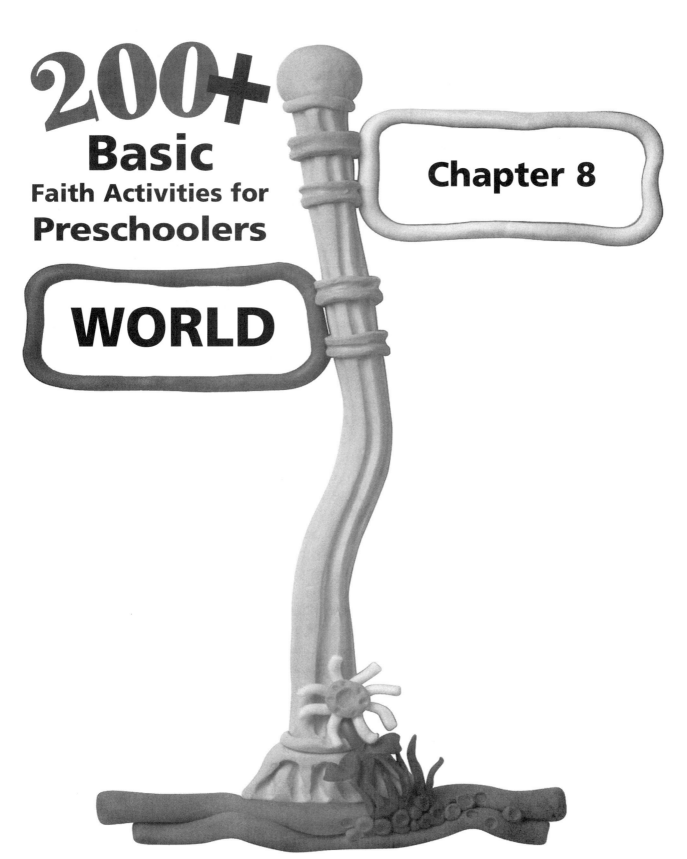

200+ Basic Faith Activities for Preschoolers

WORLD

Chapter 8

World

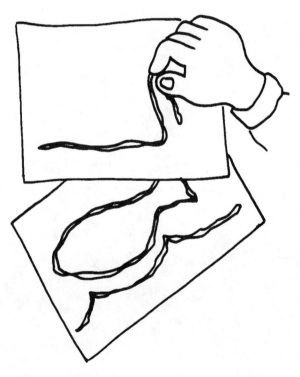

Prayer Reminders

Yarn Collage

Prayer Reminders

Materials: paper plates, colorful stickers, crayons, hole punch, 12-inch lengths of yarn

In advance, print *Today I will pray* in the middle of each paper plate. Older preschoolers may like to do this on their own.

Lead preschoolers to decorate their paper plates with the stickers and crayons. Use yarn to make a hanger at the top. Say: Hang these prayer reminders in your room or somewhere in your house to remind you to pray for the people around the world.

Open the Bible and read: Pray for one another (see James 5:16).

Music Around the World

In advance, visit your local library and check out recordings of music from various countries or ethnic groups (Chinese, African, Jamaican, Irish-Celtic, etc.).

Play recordings for preschoolers and encourage them to move to the music. Ask them what they hear. Talk about the differences in the music.

Yarn Collage

Materials: yarn, cut into several different lengths; construction paper; glue

Guide preschoolers to dip lengths of yarn into the glue, and place it on their construction paper to make all kinds of designs. Comment on the variety of designs. Say: These designs are like people—no two are exactly the same, but they are all beautiful. God loves people all over the world.

Multicultural Poster

Materials: poster board, glue, scissors, magazines with pictures of multicultural children

Help preschoolers glue the pictures showing children playing, spending time with family, going to church, and other events on the poster. As preschoolers work, talk about how we are alike and how we are different.

Open the Bible and read: A friend loves at all times (see Prov. 17:17).

An Ethnic Festival

Involve parents and family members in setting up a display of multicultural costumes and artifacts. Invite representatives of different cultures to bring a traditional food from their native country. Post the allergy notice (p. 93) if preschoolers will taste foods.

My Book of Words
Materials: paper, stapler, crayons, markers, pencils

In advance, fold several pieces of paper together. Staple the side of the paper making a basic book. Print on the front *My Book of Words*. On each of the inside pages, print one word in English and in Spanish. Make a copy for each preschooler.

Show the preschoolers a Bible and say: *Biblia* [BEE-blee-ah] is the way to say *Bible* in Spanish. The people in many countries speak Spanish.

Pronounce a word in English, then in Spanish. Suggest that each child draw a picture of the word on the page in her book.

Encourage the older preschoolers to copy the English word under the Spanish word on each page.

Some words to use are:
good morning—*buenos días* [BWAY-nohs DEE-ahs]; good-bye—*adiós* [ah-dee-OHS]; dog—*perro* [PEAR-roh]; cat—*gato* [GAH-toh]; Bible—*Biblia* [BEE-blee-ah]; I love you—*Yo te amo* [SHO teh AH-moh].

My Book of Words

What Country Do I Represent?
Materials: colorful pieces of fabric, hats, scarves, silk flowers, pictures of people of different cultures dressed in traditional clothing

In advance, gather dress-up materials for the boys and girls to pretend they are wearing clothes from different cultures.

Invite preschoolers to look at the pictures. Guide them to use the dress-up items to make an outfit that a person from another country would wear. Ask the other preschoolers to guess what country this person is from.

Around the World
Materials: multicultural tapes or CDs, maracas, tambourine, drum, castanets, scarves

Guide preschoolers to use the instruments and scarves as they move to the music. Point out areas from which a particular piece of music comes. Say: The people in Africa use the drums to make music. God loves all people.

Teaching Tip: Invite families from various cultures to share a movement activity children in their culture like to do.

Around the World

World Book

World Book
Materials: blue and green construction-paper circles, travel and news magazines, scissors, glue, large hole punch, shower curtain ring

Guide preschoolers to cut pictures of different ethnic people from magazines. Suggest they glue one picture on each round page. Punch a hole in the top, and use the shower curtain ring to bind the pages together. Share with preschoolers. Say: God loves people everywhere.

Cultural Lawn Party
Host an ethnic lawn party at church. Invite different ethnic groups in your area to attend. Let them know that this family event is to increase awareness and understanding between different cultures. Suggest that different groups wear traditional clothing, bring samples of traditional foods and music, demonstrate how to do a craft that is special to their group, and teach a traditional game. Invite the news media, and take lots of pictures. Make a contact list of individuals from each group, and share the list with all groups. Send thank-you notes, and include invitations to services offered at your church.

God Loves All People! Book

God Loves All People Book
Materials: one sheet of poster board (cut in quarters), stapler, staples, markers, glue, old magazines, scissors

Provide magazines from which preschoolers can cut photographs of all types of people. Help them cut a variety of ages, races, and ethnicities. Lead them to glue the photographs to the poster board. Title the book *God Loves All People!* Print a simple text at the bottom of each page. Say: God loves all people.
Open the Bible and read: God made us and we are His (see Psalm 100:3).

Alike and Different
In advance, take a photograph of each child and have two prints developed. Mount one set of the photographs on poster board, and laminate. Mount the second set of photographs on individual index cards, and laminate.

Invite preschoolers to choose a photograph card and match it to the correct photograph on the poster board. Ask preschoolers to name the person in each photograph. Ask: How are we alike? How are we different?

Pray and thank God for making people from all over the world.

Bulletin Board: We Are All Different

Cover the bulletin board in light blue paper. Lightly spray the paper with artificial snow. Use the Snowflake pattern on page 76 to make snowflakes. In the center of each snowflake attach a photograph of each child taken with an instant-picture camera. Mount snowflakes on the bulletin board. At the top, or center of the board, print *Like Snowflakes, We Are All Different.*

Bulletin Board

200+ Basic Faith Activities for Preschoolers

GOD'S CREATION

Chapter 9

God's Creation

Leaf Rubbings
Materials: assorted leaves with prominent veins, light-weight paper, crayons

Encourage preschoolers to examine the leaves. Guide them to feel the veins. Place the paper over the leaves and show preschoolers how to rub crayons on the paper until the leaf appears. Ask: What do you see?

Say: Thank You, God, for eyes to see.

Pretty Posies
Materials: long green chenille sticks, paper muffin-tin liners, brads, scissors

Lead preschoolers to bend their chenille sticks in half, then twist the two halves together to make a stem. Give each preschooler three muffin-tin liners. Guide them to flatten them out and color the center of one, then place it on top of the other two liners. Poke a brad through the muffin-tin liners and then through the top of the chenille stem. Spread the prongs of the brad to hold the stem to the liners. Use scissors to repeatedly make snips about 1½ inches in length, cutting through all of the liners. Bend some of the resulting petals forward and fluff others to create the look of a blossom.

Open the Bible and read: God made the flowers (see Gen. 1:11).

Pretty Posies

Butterfly Toss
Materials: disposable pie pan, construction paper, pennies, masking tape

In advance, decorate the rim of the pie pan with construction paper "petals" to look like a flower. Cut small butterflies from construction paper. Tape a penny to the back of each one to act as a weight.

Place the "flower" in the middle of the floor. Guide preschoolers to take turns standing behind a masking-tape line to toss their "butterflies" into the flower. For an added challenge, move the flower farther away.

Read with the Animals
Locate stuffed toy animals of all sizes. Try to find animals that represent those found in Africa, such as giraffes, lions, monkeys, elephants, etc. Place these in the area with books propped around them. Lead preschoolers to sit with an animal and picture-read a book.

Caution: Use only clean stuffed animals.

Butterfly Toss

Nature Weaving

Cut heavy pieces of cardboard into 12-by-12-inch pieces. Wrap lengths of yarn around the cardboard six or seven times, having about an inch between each wrap of yarn. Tape the yarn ends to the back of the cardboard.

Weather permitting, take preschoolers on a nature walk with their "looms." Encourage them to find nature items that are long enough for them to weave over and under the yarn (fern leaves, flowers, large leaves, light-weight shrub limbs, etc.).

Flower Arranging

Materials: flowers, different sizes and styles of non-breakable containers, picture of cherry blossoms in bloom

Cover the work area with newspaper. Put the materials on the newspaper. Allow preschoolers to experiment with arranging the flowers in the different containers. Encourage conversation about the colors and sizes of the flowers.

Teaching Tip: Take pictures of the preschoolers and their flower arrangements.

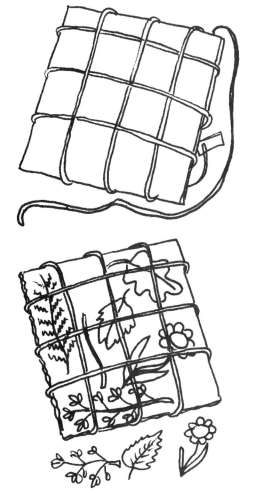

Nature Weaving

Trees, Trees, and More Trees

Materials: newsprint, sponges, 2-inch square wooden blocks, green tempera paint, shallow pan, painting smock, pictures of different types of trees

In advance, cut tree shapes from the sponges. Glue the trees onto the wooden blocks to make printing stamps.

Guide the preschoolers to put the tree stamp into the green paint, and then stamp the paper to make lots of trees.

Teaching Tip: Help preschoolers glue their pictures onto the middle of a piece of construction paper leaving a frame-like border. Print the Bible thought on the border. Allow older preschoolers to print the Bible thought on their borders.

Open the Bible and read: God made the trees (see Gen. 2:9).

Let's Go Fishing

Set up a rocking boat or a large box in an area. Prepare ten plastic fish cut out of plastic can lids. Attach a paper clip to the mouth of each fish. Make a fishing pole by tying a long string to one end of a dowel stick. Attach a magnet to the other end of the string. Add a fishing vest, hat, boots, a tackle box, and a camera.

Trees, Trees, and More Trees

What Do You Think?

What Do You Think?

Dish Garden

Teaching Tip: As preschoolers fish, sing to the tune "Ten Little Indians":

One little, two little, three little fish,
Four little, five little, six little fish,
Seven little, eight little, nine little fish,
Ten little fish swimming around the boat.

As a fish is caught, sing about the number of fish left swimming around the boat.

What Do You Think?
Materials: wood shavings, sandpaper, cotton, wool, sandpaper, tree branch or leaves; poster board; marker

In advance, make a chart with the words *hard, soft, rough,* and *smooth.* Leave space to print under each word.

Place the items on a table. Prop the chart close by. After the boys and girls have had an opportunity to handle the objects, ask them to identify each object and describe how it feels. Print the preschoolers' responses on the chart.

Dish Garden
Materials: heavy paper plates, play dough (p. 22), leaves, fresh or dry flowers, twigs, tray

Put the flowers on the tray. Place the tray and other materials on the art table.

Guide preschoolers to make a garden using the paper plate for the container. Direct the child to place a ball of play dough onto the center of the plate. Press the play dough out to the sides, filling the whole plate. Arrange different materials in the play dough to complete the garden.

Open the Bible and read: God made the flowers (see Gen. 1:11).

Moving in All Kinds of Weather
Talk about different kinds of weather. Ask each child to pretend he is a different kind of vehicle moving in one of the different weather conditions. These weather conditions include:

a dust storm
rain
snow and ice
a gentle spring breeze
a strong blowing wind

Planting Trees
Talk to someone about getting tree seedlings so each

child has one to plant. Or talk to a local nursery and ask them to donate a tree to be planted at the church. Invite someone from the nursery to visit and talk to the boys and girls about planting trees.

Wind Chimes

Materials: variety of objects, such as seashells, metal pipes, nuts, bolts; string; dowel sticks

Place the items on the nature table. Guide preschoolers to choose the items they want to use to make a wind chime. Help them tie pieces of string to each object. Next, help them tie the strings to the dowel stick. When the objects are hung, they will make a chiming sound when they bump into each other.

Suggest preschoolers hang their wind chimes outside.

Wind Chimes

Fun with Sand

Materials: shallow box, sand, glue, plastic lids, cotton swabs, lightweight poster board, plastic cups, powdered tempera paint, plastic spoons

In advance, fill plastic cups half full of sand, then add some paint. Stir the mixture together to make colored sand. Make several different colors. Cut pieces of poster board to fit inside the box.

Place a piece of poster board in the box. Put glue on a plastic lid. Direct a child to use a cotton swab dipped in the glue to draw a design on the poster board. Suggest that he sprinkle colored sand on his design. He may choose to sprinkle sand in specific places on the design rather than all over the design. Gently pick up the poster board by a corner, letting the excess sand fall back into the box. Set sand painting aside to dry.

Encourage conversation with preschoolers about their experiences of going to the beach and playing in the sand.

Fun with Sand

Sorting Rocks

Materials: an assortment of rock samples, a box with a lid, black marker

In advance, make a two-row chart inside the box lid. Place rocks in the box and cover with lid.

Invite a child to remove the lid, and look inside the box. Explain that the lid is for sorting the rocks. Tell a child that you will put various types of rocks in the squares on the top row and ask her to put the rocks of the same type in the bottom row.

Comment that some people like to hike the mountains and find special rocks.

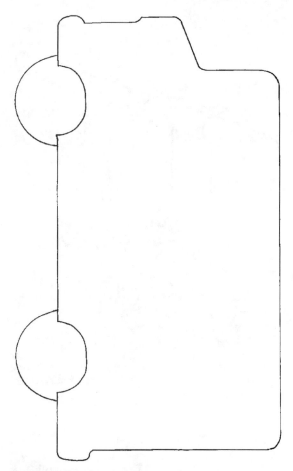
All Through the Town

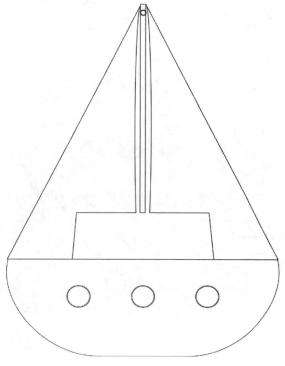
Sailing, Sailing

Open the Bible and read: Look at the wonderful things God made (see Job 37:14).

All Through the Town
Materials: construction paper; white paper; scissors; nature pictures of trees, beach, flowers, fruits, vegetables; hole punch; brad fasteners; marker; glue; enlarged bus pattern at the left

In advance, cut book cover out of colored construction paper. Enlarge and cut out several white bus shapes for the book pages. On each page, glue a picture. Put the white pages inside the book covers. Punch two holes then bind pages together with brads.

When interest is shown, invite several friends to help write a title for the book and write about each picture in the book. As the preschoolers identify the pictures, print their words on the pages. Say: Let's thank God for the things He created.

Open the Bible and read: Look at the wonderful things God made (see Job 37:14).

Teaching Tip: Provide materials for each child to make his own book.

Sailing, Sailing
Materials: construction paper, plain paper, markers, boat pattern at left, nature pictures, brad fastener

In advance, enlarge the boat pattern to make a boat-shaped book. Make book covers out of construction paper. Cut several boat-shaped pages for the inside. Bind the pages together at the mast with a brad fastener. On each page draw or glue a nature picture.

Explain to the boys and girls that their help is needed to create a story about the pictures on each page. Print their words under each picture.

Say: God made beautiful things for us to see and enjoy.

Digging Up Treasures
Materials: sand; sand table; shovel; pairs of objects, such as shells, beads, coins; index cards; tape; glue

In advance, attach one of each pair of objects on an index card. Bury the matching item in the sand.

Invite a child to use the shovel to dig for buried treasures. When he digs up a treasure, he then matches it to the one on the index card.

Thank God for the many nature treasures He gives us.

What's in the Cave?

Materials: a box large enough for a child to hide in

One child goes into the cave (box) while other friends walk very slowly around the cave chanting:

Look I see tracks. I see lots of tracks.

Look I see a cave. A big cave.

Listen I hear . . . . (child inside the cave makes a sound like an animal).

It's a _____! We better run (*walk, creep, crawl*).

What's in the Cave?

Bag Book of Colors

Materials: paper grocery sack, index cards, crayons, cutting magazines, scissors, glue

In advance, color index cards the colors red, blue, yellow, green, purple, orange, brown, black, and pink. Cut out magazine pictures of items the same colors and glue on separate cards (one picture per card). Make three cards for each color. Print each color word on an index card. Mix the cards in the bag.

Shake the bag book, and invite preschoolers to help you read it. As they take out the "pages," let them organize the book by matching color cards, picture cards, and color word cards. Say: God gives us beautiful colors to enjoy.

Looking for a Home

Materials: tagboard; markers; pictures of a whale, cow, fish, deer, goldfish, bald eagle; bag

In advance, make the gameboard. Divide a piece of tagboard into six sections. In the different sections, draw a lake, a farm, a forest, a pole by the water, ocean, and a fishbowl. Cover the gameboard and pictures with clear self-adhesive plastic. Place the pictures in the bag.

Invite a child to reach in the bag and take out a picture. Guide him to put the object in its place on the gameboard.

Looking for a Home

Snowflakes

In advance, purchase ready-made snowflakes from a teacher supply store or photocopy the pattern on page 76. Punch holes around the outside edge, and attach a long piece of ribbon to one hole. Place snowflakes, glitter glue, and scissors on a table.

Invite preschoolers to sew around a snowflake. Help them spread glitter glue on the snowflakes.

Teaching Tip: If the snowflake is one sided, print *God sends the snow (see Psalm 147:16)* on the back.

Daytime-Nighttime Pictures

Looking For Bears

Going to Market
Materials: boxes, picture of fruits and vegetables, small wheelbarrow or wagon, markers

In advance, label one box with a picture of fruit and the other box with a picture of a vegetable. Put the other pictures in the wheelbarrow.

Talk about gardens and how the farmers take the fruits and vegetables to market to sell. Ask a child to take a picture out of the wheelbarrow, name it, and decide if it goes in the fruit box or the vegetable box.
Teaching Tip: Use real fruits and vegetables for the preschoolers to sort in baskets.

Daytime-Nighttime Pictures
Materials: white paper; black paper; tape; crayons; pictures of houses, plants, and animals; star and moon shapes or stickers; glue

In advance, tape a piece of white paper and a piece of black paper together for each child. On the white paper print *Daytime* and on the black paper print *Nighttime.* (Use white crayons or markers on the black paper.)

Invite boys and girls to glue the pictures and shapes (or stickers) to make daytime and nighttime pictures.
Open the Bible and read: The sun shines in the day (see Psalm 136:8), and The moon shines in the night (see Psalm 136:9).

Looking For Bears
Materials: construction paper, marker, toy bear

In advance, cut shapes out of the construction paper and label: *glacier, snow, mountain, moose, grass,* and *trees.* Hide the bear.

Invite the boys and girls to follow you as you lead them to find the bear. As you come to an obstacle, use appropriate actions as you go through, over, or around to find the bear. Continue letting the boys and girls take turns deciding where to hide the bear and what path to take to find it.

Raindrops
Cut large raindrop shapes from construction paper. Guide preschoolers to use fingertips to spread silver glitter glue over the raindrop. Dry. Punch a hole in the top, and use yarn to hang it from the ceiling.

Provide damp paper towels to wipe fingers.
Open the Bible and read: God sends the rain (see Jer. 5:24).

Star Light, Star Bright
Materials: a paper star cutout for each child
   Give each child a paper star to stand beside. Give the following instructions:
   Star light, star bright, I'll stand beside you.
   Star light, star bright, I'll lift you high up in the sky.
   Star light, star bright, I'll jump over you.
   Continue giving instructions for ways preschoolers are to move around the star.

Greeting-Card Blocks
Materials: used greeting cards with pictures of rain, oceans, mountains, fall scenes, or people; cellophane tape; scissors; tissue paper
   In advance, select appropriate greeting cards and cut into 4-inch squares. Make a box by taping five squares together along the edges. Stuff with crumpled tissue paper. Place another card on top to form a lid and tape closed. Make several blocks.
   Invite preschoolers to build with the card blocks. Say: Which picture do you like? Why?
Open the Bible and read: Look at the wonderful things God made (see Job 37:14).

Pet Book
Gather pictures of pets from catalogs, magazines, or old photographs you have. Place pictures, glue sticks, scissors, and construction paper on a table. Ask preschoolers to choose a picture of a pet they would like to have, cut it out, and glue it on a piece of paper. On another page, print *Look at the wonderful things God made (see Job 37:14).* Put together and staple the left edge of the book. Share the book.

Wildlife Animal Figures
Lead preschoolers to help cut wildlife animal pictures from outdoors and wildlife magazines. Look for deer, elk, bighorn sheep, moose, mountain lions, coyote, and bears. Mount them on construction paper and tape to wooden blocks. Arrange in an area.
   As preschoolers enjoy the animals, say: God made the animals.

Homemade Trees
Materials: lids from hair spray or starch cans; plaster of Paris; water; sticks, thin branches, or shrub clippings; allergy alert chart (p. 93)

Star Light, Star Bright

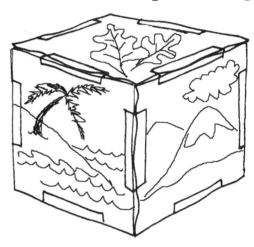

Greeting-Card Blocks

Look at the wonderful things God made (see Job 37:14).

Pet Book

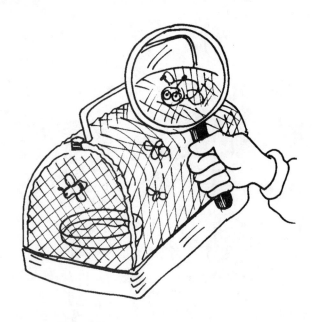

Bug Zoo

Window Book

In advance, break sticks, branches, and shrub clippings into pieces about 10 inches long. Place one in each lid. With the help of a friend, mix plaster of Paris, and pour into each lid, holding the tree upright. Prop against a wall to harden. Post the allergy alert chart.

Point to the trees, and say: God made the trees.

Bug Zoo

Borrow an insect cage, or make one by cutting the sides out of a shoe box and covering the openings with window screen. Catch or purchase insects or crickets. Place a shallow lid inside with water. Place the cage and a magnifying glass on a table.

Invite preschoolers to examine the insects in the cage. Talk about insects. Ask why these insects can't get out. Say: God made animals, even bugs!

Window Book

Materials: large pieces of flat cardboard, clear vinyl, glue gun, colorful fabric

Cut an 11-by-17 rectangle from cardboard. Cut a piece of clear vinyl slightly smaller and glue the bottom and the sides to the cardboard with the glue gun. Leave the top open to form a pocket. Cut a piece of fabric the same size as cardboard. Cut down the center of the fabric to make curtains. Glue the curtains to the top edge of the cardboard.

Use picture file pictures. Place a picture in the pocket, and close the curtains. Ask preschoolers to guess what is behind the curtains. Look. Let preschoolers tell the story of the picture.

Open the Bible and read: Look at the wonderful things God made (see Job 37:14).

I Am Thankful Book

Materials: construction paper; stapler and staples; photographs or pictures of snow, pine trees, beach, flowers, grass, family.

In advance, place one photo or picture in the center of each page. Cover each photo with a construction-paper door that opens to reveal the photo. Above each photo print the phrase *Am I thankful? Yes!* Below each photo, print the phrase *Thank You, God, for (item).*

Read the book to preschoolers. Ask them to guess what is behind each door. When you finish reading, ask them to name something for which they are thankful.

Teaching Tip: Point to words as you read. This helps preschoolers learn to read from left to right.

Pine Tree

In advance, draw a large pine tree on green butcher paper. Tape large paper clips all over the tree. Attach loops of yarn to the branch ends of several pinecones. Drop the pinecones on the floor. Place a basket nearby.

Invite preschoolers to use the basket and gather pinecones. After they have gathered them all, hook them on the tree by placing the loop over a paper clip. Pick the pinecones.

Pine Tree

Nature Sounds

Materials: recording of birds chirping, dogs barking, cat meowing, rain falling, wind blowing

Play the recording. Challenge preschoolers to identify what each sound represents.

For an added challenge, ask older preschoolers to draw one of the things they heard on the recording.
Open the Bible and read: God gave us ears to hear (see Prov. 20:12).

Sequencing Trees

From construction paper, cut out five trees that are each a different size. Mix up the sizes, and spread on a table. Invite preschoolers to put them in order from smallest to biggest. When a child is done, mix them up and ask someone else to put them in order from biggest to smallest.

Sequencing Trees

What's Inside the Bag?

Materials: brown paper bags; various nature items (seashell, leaf, rock, blades of grass)

In advance, place one nature item in each brown paper bag. Invite preschoolers to take turns reaching into each bag and guessing what is inside. Ask: What does it feel like? What do you think is in the bag?

Show preschoolers the item. Say: God makes the grass grow. He makes the beach. He makes leaves and rocks. Thank You, God, for the wonderful things You made!

Mitten Match

Bring a variety of pairs of winter mittens and gloves. Encourage preschoolers to help you find the ones that match to make a pair. Ask: Why are two mittens alike? (We need one mitten for each hand.).

If time permits, allow preschoolers to try on the mittens and gloves.
Open the Bible and read: God made the winter (see Psalm 74:17).

What's Inside the Bag?

Winter Book

Winter Book

Make a winter book on blue construction paper (cut in half). Cut winter pictures from old calendars, greeting cards, and magazines. Glue one picture on each page, and tape together accordion fashion on the long sides. Stand the winter book zigzag on a table. Invite preschoolers to read the pages.

Shell Book

Shell Book

Cut several same-sized shell shapes from construction paper. Draw lines like a shell on the first one. On the second page, print *God made the ocean and the dry land (see Psalm 95:5).* On additional pages, add photos or magazine pictures of beaches and beach activities (swimmers, shells, sunset, horseback riders, and so on). Include pictures of your family at the beach. Bind at the top with two metal rings through punched holes.

Read the book with preschoolers. Before turning the pages, read the Bible thought and let preschoolers predict what will be in the book.

Make It Rain

In advance, prepare empty tin cans by punching holes in the bottom with an awl and hammer. Make one per child.

Take boys and girls outside to make it rain on plants. Using a bucket of water, let preschoolers scoop out water, and then walk around making it rain (dripping water out of their cans) onto plants. Say: The rain helps the plants grow.

Make It Rain

Leaf Concentration Game

In advance, collect leaves. Be sure to gather two leaves that are similar in appearance from each tree. Mount each leaf on a small square of construction paper.

Place all squares facedown on a table. Ask preschoolers to turn over two squares to see if the two leaves are alike. Suggest preschoolers take turns continuing to turn over two leaves at a time until all matches are found. Say: God gives us beautiful colors on the leaves.

Raindrops or Snowflakes Finger Play

Sing or chant "Raindrops" and do a finger play.

Ten little raindrops dancing on the walk, (tap fingers on floor).

Pitter patter, pitter patter, that's the way they talk (tap fingers on floor).

Out comes the yellow sun shining in the sky (make a large circle with fingers for the sun).
And away all the raindrops fly, fly, fly (quickly hide fingers behind back).
Change the words from *raindrops* to *snowflakes*.

Cloud and Rain Mobile

Materials: blue construction paper, white or gray construction paper, scissors, yarn or string, hole punch, crayons, glue

In advance, enlarge and prepare each child one white or gray cloud and three blue raindrops using the patterns at right. Punch one hole near the top of the clouds and three holes near the bottom edge. Print the Bible thought, *God makes the rain (see Psalm 147:8)* on each cloud. Punch one hole near the top of each raindrop cutout.

Help preschoolers tie a piece of yarn through the top of the cloud. Read the Bible thought together. Say: Rain helps people, animals, and plants. Thank You, God, for rain.

Give each preschooler three raindrops. Encourage them to tie their raindrops onto the bottom of the cloud to complete their mobile.

Cloudy with a Chance Of Snow Book

Materials: *Cloudy with a Chance of Meatballs* by Judi Barrett (classic children's book available in public library), cotton balls, glue, construction paper, markers and crayons, stapler and staples

Read the silly story to preschoolers. Ask them what might really fall from the sky (rain, hail, snow). Give each preschooler a piece of construction paper to make a snow scene using the cotton balls.

Staple the completed pages together. Title the book *Cloudy with a Chance of Snow.* Encourage preschoolers to tell you about their pictures.
Open the Bible and read: God sends the snow (see Psalm 147:16).

Clouds and Raindrops

Materials: white construction paper, marker, scissors, gray construction paper, clear self-adhesive plastic (for laminating)

Make five clouds from white construction paper. Write a numeral from 1 to 5 on each cloud. Make 15 raindrops out of gray construction paper. Laminate both the clouds and the raindrops. Help preschoolers

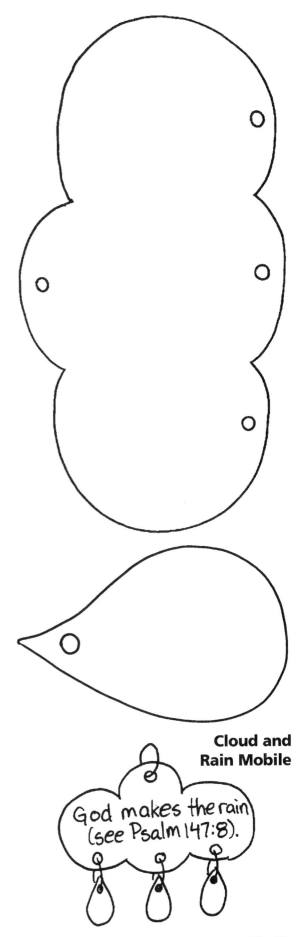

Cloud and Rain Mobile

count the corresponding number of raindrops onto each cloud.

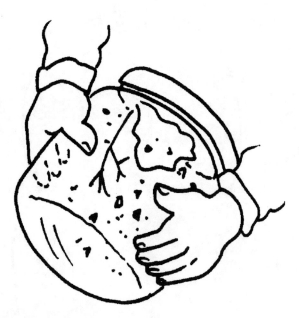

Snow Scene in a Jar

Snow Scene in a Jar
Materials: empty small jars with lids (such as baby food jars), hot glue gun, epoxy glue, small plastic toy animals , white rocks, plastic trees, glitter, water, food coloring (if desired)

Invite preschoolers to select some white rocks and an animal. An adult should use a hot glue gun to glue rocks and the animal to the lid. Lead preschoolers to fill their jars with water and add food coloring if desired. Spoon in some glitter and use epoxy glue to secure the lid onto jar. Turn over and shake to make it snow! Say: God sends the snow.
Caution: Be sure an adult helps with the epoxy glue. Supervise carefully.

Snowy Picture Puzzles
Materials: snow scenes from old greeting cards or calendars, scissors, glue, heavy poster board, self-sealing plastic sandwich bags

In advance, find snow-scene pictures and mount to poster board. Cut each picture into four to six pieces, and place each picture puzzle in a separate plastic sandwich bag.

Place the bags on a table and help preschoolers work the puzzles.
Open the Bible and read: God sends the snow (see Psalm 147:16).

Snowy Picture Puzzles

Sunny Streamers
Materials: yellow paint, yellow streamers, glue, large circles cut from plain paper

Lead preschoolers to paint large circles with yellow paint. When the paint has dried, they can glue short yellow streamers around the edges of their sunny circles. Say: The sun shines a lot in summer. God made the sun, and God made the summer.
Open the Bible and read: God made the summer (see Psalm 74:17).

Tornado in a Jar

Materials: clear plastic, 1-quart jar with lid; liquid dishwashing soap; food coloring (preferably green)

In advance, fill the jar with water and put a few drops of dishwashing soap in the jar. Then put a few drops of food coloring in the jar. Put the lid on tight.

As preschoolers watch, swirl the jar in a circular motion several times, and then stop and look inside the jar. **Be certain the outside of the jar is dry and hold onto the jar tightly.** You should see what looks like a tornado. The tornado will slowly disappear as it moves upward towards the top of the jar. Repeat as many times as you would like.

Tornado in a Jar

Fingerprint Insects

Materials: washable stamp pads, paper, colored pens

Lead preschoolers to put their fingers on a stamp pad and press them carefully on paper. They can use pens to add eyes, noses, mouths, antennae, and ears. Preschoolers may choose to make a special card from their fingerprint insects.

Fingerprint Insects

Summer Sunshine Finger Play

Teach preschoolers the following finger play and do it several times.

> The sun makes the outside a warm place to play
> (arms above head in circle).
> It makes the flowers grow each day (holding up hands wiggling fingers).
> The sun hides during the night (cover face with hands).
> But during the daytime it shines—oh so bright (arms above head in circle).

Summer Sunshine Finger Play

Bulletin Board

Cut letters from red construction paper to make the phrase *Look at all the wonderful things God made (see Job 37:14).* Cover the bulletin board with blue paper. Place the red letters on the bulletin board. Display a spring nature scene, including a pond, mother and baby animals, children, flowers blooming, tree budding, and bird singing. Attach pictures of preschoolers' faces to the bulletin board to serve as a border or intersperse them throughout the scene.

Bulletin Board

Look at all the wonderful things God made (see Job 37:14).

Allergy Alert Chart
Look what preschoolers are doing!

We will _____

_____

_____

_____

_____

_____

If your child is allergic to any of these items, please sign his/her name below.

Child's Name

_____

_____

_____

_____

_____

Allergic to

_____

_____

_____

_____

_____

Photocopy and laminate to reuse. Use a grease pencil or washable marker to note items used in a session.

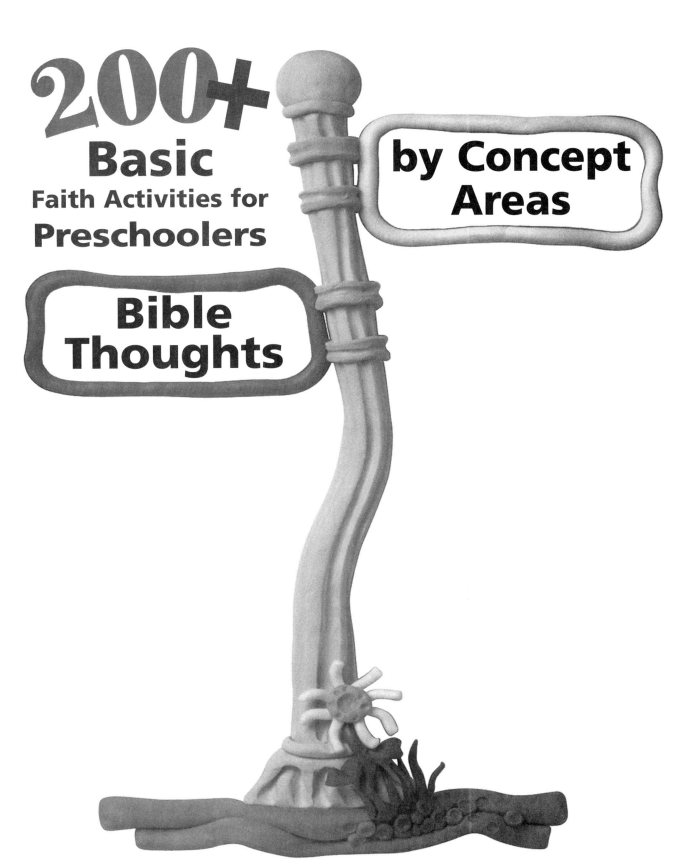

200+ Basic Faith Activities for Preschoolers

Bible Thoughts

by Concept Areas

Notes

These are simplified paraphrases of Bible verses, written specifically for use with preschoolers. You won't find the exact same wording in any translation of the Bible. Some verses are used in more than one concept area, since they can apply in several different situations.

Bible

• The Bible is useful for teaching us how to live (see 2 Timothy 3:16).

• All that the Bible says is from God (see 2 Timothy 3:16).

Church

• I will sing to God (see Exodus 15:1).

• Bring an offering (see 1 Chronicles 16:29).

• Be glad and sing songs to God (see Psalm 9:2).
  I will be glad and sing songs to God (see Psalm 9:2).
  I will be glad and sing praise to God (see Psalm 9:2).

• Sing praises to God (see Psalm 47:6).

• I will praise God with a song (see Psalm 69:30).

• It is a good thing to give thanks to God (see Psalm 92:1).

• Give thanks to God and praise him (see Psalm 100:4).

• Give thanks to the Lord for he is good (see Psalm 107:1).
  God loves us (see Psalm 107:1).
  God loves us always (see Psalm 107:1).

• I like to go to church (see Psalm 122:1).
  I was glad when they said, "Let us go to church" (see Psalm 122:1).

• Sing thanks to God (see Psalm 147:7).

• Bring an offering to church (see Malachi 3:10).

• Jesus went to church (see Luke 4:16).

• We work together (see 1 Corinthians 3:9).

• We are helpers (see 2 Corinthians 1:24).

• God loves a cheerful giver (see 2 Corinthians 9:7).

• Help one another (see Galatians 5:13).
  Be kind to each other (see Ephesians 4:32).
  We give thanks to God (see Colossians 1:3).

- I thank God (see 2 Timothy 1:3).

- Pray for one another (see James 5:16).

- Love one another (see 1 John 4:7).

Family

- Love your father and mother (see Exodus 20:12).

- Jesus' family went to church (see Luke 2:27).

- Love each other (see John 15:17).

- We work together (see 1 Corinthians 3:9).

- We are helpers (see 2 Corinthians 1:24).

- Help one another (see Galatians 5:13).

- Be kind to each other (see Ephesians 4:32).

- Children, obey your parents (see Colossians 3:20).

- Pray for one another (see James 5:16).

- Love one another (see 1 John 4:7).

God

- God made the flowers (see Genesis 1:11).
  (fruit, grass, trees, also may be used)

- God made the moon (see Genesis 1:16).
  (sun, stars may also be used)

- God made the birds (see Genesis 1:21).
  (fish may also be used)

- God made the cows (see Genesis 1:25).

- God made people (see Genesis 1:27).
  God made man (see Genesis 1:27).
  God made woman (see Genesis 1:27).
  God made man and woman (see Genesis 1:27).

- God looked at everything he had made and he was very pleased
  (see Genesis 1:31).
  Everything God made was very good (see Genesis 1:31).
  God saw everything that He had made, and it was very good
  (see Genesis 1:31).

- God made the trees (see Genesis 2:9).

- I will sing to God (see Exodus 15:1).

- Look at the wonderful things God made (see Job 37:14).

- Be glad and sing songs to God (see Psalm 9:2).
  I will be glad and sing songs to God (see Psalm 9:2).
  I will be glad and sing praise to God (see Psalm 9:2).
  Sing praises to God (see Psalm 47:6).

- I will praise God with a song (see Psalm 69:30).

- God is good to us (see Psalm 73:1).

- God made the summer (see Psalm 74:17).
  (winter may also be used)

- It is a good thing to give thanks to God (see Psalm 92:1).

- God made the ocean and the dry land (see Psalm 95:5).

- God made us and we are his (see Psalm 100:3).
  The Lord is good (see Psalm 100:3).

- Give thanks to God and praise him (see Psalm 100:4).

- God made the water (see Psalm 104:10).

- Give thanks to the Lord for he is good (see Psalm 107:1).
  God loves us (see Psalm 107:1).
  God loves us always (see Psalm 107:1).

- Say thank you to God (see Psalm 136:1).

- God made me (see Psalm 139:14).

- Sing thanks to God (see Psalm 147:7).

- God makes the wind blow (see Psalm 147:18).

- God sends the rain (see Jeremiah 5:24).

- God made the grasshopper (see Amos 7:1).

- Love God (see Mark 12:30).
  Love God very much (see Mark 12:30).

- Look what God can do (see Luke 1:37).

- God made the world (see Acts 17:24).

- God loves a cheerful giver (see 2 Corinthians 9:7).

- God gives us things to enjoy (see 1 Timothy 6:17).

- I thank God (see 2 Timothy 1:3).

- God cares for you (see 1 Peter 5:7).

- God loves us (see 1 John 4:10).
  God loved us and sent his Son (see 1 John 4:10).

Jesus

- Jesus was born in Bethlehem (see Matthew 2:1).

- Jesus lived in Nazareth (see Matthew 2:23).

- Jesus talked to God (see Matthew 14:23).
  Jesus prayed (see Matthew 14:23).
  Jesus prayed when he was alone (see Matthew 14:23).

- Jesus said, "Let the children come to me" (see Matthew 19:14).

- Jesus' family went to church (see Luke 2:27).

- Jesus grew and became strong (see Luke 2:40).

- Jesus grew (see Luke 2:52).

- Jesus went to church (see Luke 4:16).

- Jesus taught the people (see Luke 5:3).

- Jesus made blind people see (see Luke 7:21).
  Jesus made sick people well (see Luke 7:21).

- Jesus said, "I love you" (see John 15:9).

- Jesus loves you (see John 15:12).

- Jesus said, "You are my friends" (see John 15:14).

- Jesus said, "Love one another" (see John 15:17).
  Love each other (see John 15:17).

- Jesus went about doing good (see Acts 10:38).

- God loved us and sent his Son (see 1 John 4:10).

God's Creation

- God called the light day and the darkness he called night (see Genesis 1:5).

- God made the flowers (see Genesis 1:11). (fruit, grass, trees, also may be used)

- God made the moon (see Genesis 1:16). (sun, stars may also be used)

- God made the birds (see Genesis 1:21). (fish may also be used)

- God made the cows (see Genesis 1:25). (animals may also be used)

- God made people (see Genesis 1:27). God made man (see Genesis 1:27). God made woman (see Genesis 1:27). God made man and woman (see Genesis 1:27).

- God looked at everything he had made and he was very pleased (see Genesis 1:31). Everything God made was very good (see Genesis 1:31). God saw everything that He had made, and it was very good (see Genesis 1:31).

- God made the trees (see Genesis 2:9).

- God made the clouds (see Job 36:27) (rain to fall)

- Look at the wonderful things God made (see Job 37:14).

- God made the summer (see Psalm 74:17). (winter may also be used)

- God made the ocean and the dry land (see Psalm 95:5).

- The Lord is good (see Psalm 100:3). God made us and we are his (see Psalm 100:3).

- God made the water (see Psalm 104:10). (rivers)

- God makes the grass grow (see Psalm 104:14).

- The birds make their nests (see Psalm 104:17).

- God makes darkness and it is night (see Psalm 104:20).

- The sun shines in the day (see Psalm 136:8).

- The moon shines in the night (see Psalm 136:9). (stars may be used)

- God gives food to us (see Psalm 136:25).

- God makes rain (see Psalm 147:8).

- God makes the grass grow (see Psalm 147:8).

- God gives food to animals (see Psalm 147:9). (birds may also be used)

- God sends the snow (see Psalm 147:16). (frost)

- God makes the wind blow (see Psalm 147:18).

- Everything God made is beautiful (see Ecclesiastes 3:11).

- The flowers grow (see Song of Solomon 2:12).

- The time of the singing of birds has come (see Song of Solomon 2:12).

- God sends the rain (see Jeremiah 5:24).

- God makes the lightning flash (see Jeremiah 10:13).

- God gives the moon and stars to shine in the night (see Jeremiah 31:35).
  God made the sun, the moon and the stars (see Jeremiah 31:35).
  The sun shines in the day (see Jeremiah 31:35).

- God made the grasshopper (see Amos 7:1).

- God makes his sun rise (see Matthew 5:45).

- The birds have nests (see Matthew 8:20).

- God gives us things to enjoy (see 1 Timothy 6:17).

Community/World

- God is good to us (see Psalm 73:1).

- God made us (see Psalm 100:3).
  The Lord is good (see Psalm 100:3).
  God made us and we are his (see Psalm 100:3).

Notes

- A friend loves at all times (see Proverbs 17:17).

- Jesus had friends (see Luke 2:52).

- Jesus said, "You are my friends" (see John 15:14).

- Jesus said, "Love one another" (see John 15:17).
  Love each other (see John 15:17).

- We work together (see 1 Corinthians 3:9).

- We are helpers (see 2 Corinthians 1:24).

- Help one another (see Galatians 5:13).

- Be kind to each other (see Ephesians 4:32).

- Pray for one another (see James 5:16).

- Love one another (see 1 John 4:7).

Self

- God made people (see Genesis 1:27).
  God made man (see Genesis 1:27).
  God made woman (see Genesis 1:27).
  God made man and woman (see Genesis 1:27).

- I will sing to God (see Exodus 15:1).

- Be glad and sing songs to God (see Psalm 9:2).
  I will be glad and sing songs to God (see Psalm 9:2).
  I will be glad and sing praise to God (see Psalm 9:2).

- I will praise God with a song (see Psalm 69:30).

- God is good to us (see Psalm 73:1).

- It is a good thing to give thanks to God (see Psalm 92:1).

- God made us (see Psalm 100:3).
  God made us and we are his (see Psalm 100:3).
  The Lord is good (see Psalm 100:3).

- Give thanks to the Lord for he is good (see Psalm 107:1).
  God loves us (see Psalm 107:1).
  God loves us always (see Psalm 107:1).

- I like to go to church (see Psalm 122:1).

- Give thanks to God (see Psalm 136:1).

- God gives food to us (see Psalm 136:25).

- God made me (see Psalm 139:14).
  I am wonderfully made (see Psalm 139:14).

- Sing praises to God (see Psalm 147:6).

- Sing thanks to God (see Psalm 147:7).

- God gave us ears to hear (see Proverbs 20:12).
  God gave us eyes to see (see Proverbs 20:12).
  God gave us ears to hear and eyes to see (see Proverbs 20:12).

- Love God (see Mark 12:30).
  Love God very much (see Mark 12:30).

- Jesus said, "I love you" (see John 15:9).

- Jesus said, "You are my friends" (see John 15:14).

- Love each other (see John 15:7).

- We work together (see 1 Corinthians 3:9).

- We are helpers (see 2 Corinthians 1:24).

- Help one another (see Galatians 5:13).

- We give thanks to God (see Colossians 1:3).

- Work with your hands (see 1 Thessalonians 4:11).

- I thank God (see 2 Timothy 1:3).

- Pray for one another (see James 5:16).

- God cares for you (see 1 Peter 5:7).

- Love one another (see 1 John 4:7).

- God loves us (see 1 John 4:10).
  God loved us and sent his Son (see 1 John 4:10).

Also in the
200+ series

200+ Games and Fun Activities
for Teaching Preschoolers
0-93662-570-8

200+ Ideas for Teaching
Preschoolers
0-93662-506-6

200+ Things to Make
for Teaching Preschoolers
1-56309-019-8

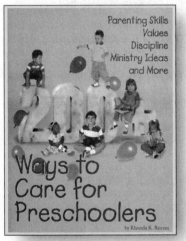

200+ Ways to Care
for Preschoolers
1-56309-208-5

Available in Christian bookstores everywhere.

new
hope
PUBLISHERS

Inspiring Women. Changing Lives.